Ex Libris

The Sound of Ving Tsun
The Grandmasters and Masters

Second  Edition

2023

First Edition
2004

THE SOUND OF VING TSUN
The Grandmasters and Masters

Darrell Jordan

World Ving Tsun Association
World Ving Tsun.com

The Sound of Ving Tsun - The Grandmasters and Masters, by Darrell Jordan, Copyright © First Edition 2004, Second Edition 2023. All rights reserved.

No part of this book may be reproduced in whole or in part without the written permission from the publisher, nor stored in any retrieval system or transmitted by any means, electronic, mechanical, photocopying, recording, or other, without the written consent of the publisher.

For bulk purchases, please contact the publisher.
Enquiry@Athenaia.Co

Library of Congress Cataloging-in Publication Data
Names: Jordan, Darrell
Title: The Sound of Ving Tsun: The Grandmasters and Masters / Darrell Jordan
Description: Second U.S. edition. | Coeur D'Alene, Idaho: Athenaia [2023]
Identifiers: LCCN (pending) | ISBN 978-0-9728825-4-5 (First Edition paperback) | ISBN 979-8-88556-030-6 (Second Edition hardcover)
Subjects: SPO02700: SPORTS & RECREATION | Martial Arts | General, | BIO026000: BIOGRAPHY & AUTOBIOGRAPHY | Personal Memoirs
LC record available at https://lccn. loc.gov

On the internet: World Ving Tsun.com
Managing Editor: Darrell Jordan
Production Editor: Yuka Jordan
Book Cover Design by Justyn Rowe, Yuka Jordan
Photography Credits: Darrell Jordan, William Wong, Chan Chee Man, Chu Shong Tin, Buick Yip, Donald Mak, Judy Chan

Articles reprinted with permission:
KungFuMagazine.com
Chan Chee Man: Sept. 2001; Siu Yuk Men: Mar. 2002
Journal of Chinese Martial Arts
Chow Tze Chuen: Summer 2001

Printed and bound in the United States

Publisher: Athenaia
2370 N Merritt Crk Lp, Ste 1
Coeur D'Alene, ID 83814
The United States
Enquiry@Athenaia.Co

This book is not for instructional purposes and is not intended to replace a qualified instructor in Ving Tsun Kung Fu. Opinions on medical or health matters are not necessarily those of or endorsed by the publisher and are only the opinion of the interviewed. It is advisable to seek medical advice before starting any exercise program.

DISCLAIMER

Any mistakes regarding interpretation of the dialogue with those that were interviewed are solely mine. Note, I did not change the flavor of their speech. I wanted to impart to the reader the words as they were presented to me.

THE WORLD VING TSUN ASSOCIATION

Dedicated to the Memories of Grandmaster Moy Yat 1938 – 2001

Grandmaster Chan Chee Man 1936 – 2022

ACKNOWLEDGEMENTS

I would like to thank my Sigung Grandmaster Moy Yat who provided the correct path for so many. Rest in Peace, Sigung.

To grandmaster Chan Chee Man for sharing his friendship, knowledge and in support of the WVTA as chairman.

Sifu Lee Moy Shan who shined the light for those of us who wanted to see.

The Grandmasters and Masters themselves, for sharing their wisdom.

My Kung Fu brothers Steve Goericke, Vinny Thomas, Richie Louie, and Paul Field for their guidance in Ving Tsun.

My Kung Fu Uncle Moy 29 for all of the energy that he spent on my personal kung fu development.

To all of my students, from whom I have learned even as they learned from me.

My Sihing Buick Yip for his assistance and patience with the Gwailo's during our visit to Hong Kong.

My Todai Brian McDonald for getting me there, and for all his assistance on this project.

My late Todai Dave Catapano (Lee Yi Kai) who's faith continues to inspire me.

Last but never least; I extend my appreciation to Sidai Steve Faber M.D. for his helping hand with this book.

And to all who follow the Ving Tsun path.

INTRODUCTION

When my Sigung passed away in 2001, I realized that Ving Tsun's most valuable teachers were gaining in age and gradually leaving us. In the hope of preserving as much of their perspective and expertise as possible, my Disciple (Todai) Brian McDonald and I visited Hong Kong and interviewed the Grandmasters that March. Ving Tsun is very popular in North America and Europe but very few of the grandmasters live abroad, so most are not privileged to receive instruction from them. Nonetheless, I believe you will sense these men's power and the very spirit of Ving Tsun in their words [here].

Except for some of my subjects' training with Yip Man, I stayed away from historical matters in our conversations. Over the years alternative history has been presented and while these stories may be interesting, in the end I find they do nothing for my Kung Fu. Most of my questions pertain to the concepts of attacking and defending, and of fighting in general, the topics of primary interest to most students. Even so, the final interview, with Lee Moy Shan Sifu, is especially philosophical. He reminds us that Ving Tsun can guide us through our lives outside the gym, developing our compassion for our fellow human beings and even aiding us in our professional lives. This martial art's scope is far broader than most beginners ever imagined.

Ving Tsun Kung Fu works its way into a student and hooks him. I know of no other martial art system that so often leaves every student smiling at the end of class. The constant smacking and pounding on the arms and legs takes a little time to grow accustomed to and will discourage some of the toughest from continuing. But once past that stage, a student realizes there is nothing in the world like Ving Tsun Kung Fu.

A Ving Tsun fighter uncovers his opponent's intentions through their contact and so controls him, a fascinating concept. In Chi Sao one refines the continual flow of the arms, hands and legs from one strategic position to another. The fighter with the superior position can hit without being hit. Whenever one uses his energy inappropriately, an opening appears and he is hit.

Ving Tsun requires diligence, consistency and patience, and many beginners are unwilling to invest the necessary time. You will sweat and experience some soreness, but in the end your work will transform you. This martial art is not strictly about self-defense; it's about living, so live a little.

Ving Tsun is aptly called the thinking man's art: once it is in your bones; you think about it all of the time. How can these simple positions and small movements be so effective? The question lingers in your mind as you perpetually work out the systems nuances. Of course, the easiest answer lies in geometry, where leverage is discovered. If you understand leverage, you do not have to be stronger than your opponent to defeat him.

The combined experience of the men I interviewed for this book total over 300 years, nearly as many as Ving Tsun has existed. All of these Grandmasters and Masters hail from the Yip Man lineage, but each understands this system in their own way. Likewise, The Ving Tsun you learn becomes you, you do not become it. Grandmaster Moy Yat's advice expresses this phenomenon perfectly:
"Enslave yourself to Ving Tsun, and then free yourself from it."

I hope you find as much value in these interviews as I have. Experiment with the knowledge learned from them in your own way and use it to your own advantage. In the end, all that is left is to grow. The key to your growth in Ving Tsun is effective application of your imagination; the observations and stories of the Grandmasters and Masters are food for your imagination.

2023 Addendum to the Introduction

With the passing of Grandmaster Chan Chee Man in 2022 – Chairman of the World Ving Tsun Association, I was at a loss for words. The sorrow I felt affected me tremendously, his passing was a tragic loss to the Ving Tsun family worldwide and to martial arts in general.

It was most fortunate that I had the foresight to publish this book when I did and is what motivated me to publish this 2nd edition of *The Sound of Ving Tsun*. The second edition, now in hardback includes not only B&W pictures but color pictures as well. The purpose of this was to better ensure its existence for readers in the future. Also, one additional interview has been added. I'm proud to feature Dr. Wong Moy Ping (25) (William Wong) from the old Moy Yat - Ding Leg school in Brooklyn NY. Dr. Wong does not hold back nor minces his words when it comes to Ving Tsun.

Thank you and enjoy.

Back Row L-R: Author, Brian McDonald, Wu Chun Nam, Andrew Ma, Chu Shong Tin, Chan Chee Man, Chow Tze Chuen, Siu Yuk Men, Lee Wai Chi - Bottom Row L-R: Steve Goericke, Donald Mak, Cliff Au Yeung, Chiu Hok Yin, unknown, Buick Yip, Lewis Luk, Lee Moy Shan – Luncheon with the Grandmasters and Masters in honor of GM Moy Yat.

Table of Contents

Dedicated to the Memories of _____ iii

Grandmaster Moy Yat 1938 – 2001 _____ iii

Grandmaster Chan Chee Man 1936 – 2022 _____ iii

ACKNOWLEDGEMENTS _____ v

INTRODUCTION _____ vii

2023 Addendum to the Introduction _____ viii

CHAN CHEE MAN _____ 3

CHU SHONG TIN _____ 19

CHOW TZE CHUEN _____ 31

SIU YUK MEN _____ 45

WU CHUN NAM _____ 57

CLIFF AU YEUNG _____ 65

DONALD MAK _____ 77

LEWIS LUK _____ 95

LEE MOY SHAN _____ 109

DR. WONG MOY PING _____ 145

About the Author _____ 163

Other Products by the Author _____ 174

"Your Hands and Feet Develop a Mind of Their Own."

CHAN CHEE MAN

L-R Standing: Sihing Buick Yip, Author with Grandmaster Chan Chee Man and Mrs. Chan.

DJ: Could you tell us how you became interested in Ving Tsun?

CCM: I remember about 45 years ago; I was very young at the time. Before Ving Tsun, I knew Choy Li Fut. So, I knew William Cheung and one day I asked him to play the Ving Tsun boxing, let me see it I said, and he just played the Siu Nim Tao (Little Idea form). Siu Nim Tao is nothing in my eyes, just like that Tan Sao, Fuk Sao, how can you hit the people? So, I said, "OK, William Cheung, I can play with you." Actually, he is a fighter, he said, "I have no time today, maybe next day."

After 2 days, he brings up almost 20 friends. I brought nearly 10 friends, so we go to the roof and we start to play. William Cheung is in Bai Jong (Ready position) and I attack him, and so he socked me with a straight punch. So, I try to push down his hands and cannot. When I try to push down his hand, the other would come up to punch. So, I nearly fall off the roof, luckily, there was a pole for the flag, and I saved myself by grabbing on. All during that night, my chest was hurting. So, I go to the Dit Da Bruise-hit) Doctor. After that I still did not have enough because I think he cannot always hit me like this, when it is so basic.

So next time I ask William Cheung to fight again, but this time we bring no friends.

I warn him not to hit too heavy because I was hurt already. So, this time up I thought I was very clear. So I fight him again, and twice I end up with no where to go, so I was very disappointed. So, I said, "OK, where you learn this from?" He said the restaurant workers union, so I said, "you bring me there." But actually, I don't know Sifu called Yip Man, I don't know at all. So, I just learn Ving Tsun, I don't care who is teaching me. So, when I have the Siu Nim Tao, Tan Sao, Fuk Sao, I still don't know who Yip Man is.

So, one day, I go back to my former teacher, he told me if you learn Ving Tsun, you must follow Yip Man he is the best one. The next day, I saw William Cheung, and I tell him that Ving Tsun Sifu Yip Man is the best.

He starts laughing, he said, "you are silly, that is Yip Man." I don't believe it, so we get a taxi and go to the union, and face the Sifu, "are you Yip Man?" He says nothing, and is just laughing. But since then, I feel very very interested in learning the Ving Tsun. I remember that I practice the Siu Nim Tao for quite a long time, a month and a half just doing Siu Nim Tao.

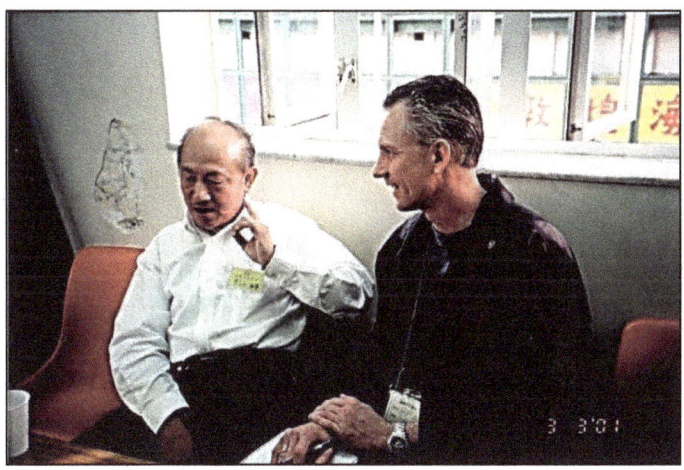

At the Hong Kong VTAA.

Batt Jom Doa in the home of GM Chan.

I remember Sifu always come around when I'm tired and say, "Oh, go ahead and play Siu Nim Tao again. "I never complain that he teach me too slow, never.

Because at that time, I really liked the Ving Tsun. So, every night we go to the union to practice from 7 to half past 9. After half past 9, Yip Man Sifu would go to the temple. At the temple, Sifu met the Tong Jong students, the older students to practice. So, at the temple, there was a wall, and there was another guy that taught another style kung fu. So, William Cheung at that time was very naughty, and another guy, I can't remember who. We used to climb up the wall and watch. How could other people learn this kung fu? We used to laugh and talk about it. So, we are hiding on the wall, and then Sifu would pass by. So, one of Sifu's Todai's met him on the street and spoke to him. Yip Man Sifu got very angry, he goes in the temple and says, "who climb up the wall and watch the people, and say something?" I and William Cheung knew it was us.

Since then, Yip Man said no one is to climb up the wall. Yip Man taught us a lot you know. He taught us the Ving Tsun action. He said the Ving Tsun action is like a cat. The cat catch a mouse, he wait for the mouse to pass in front, and spring onto the mouse. It is what he called the gate. When it enters the gate, go. He taught us about being soft. Teach how to chase the body, also, you must take one side of the opponent's body, put both arms to one side. You must use bridge close to their elbows to control, and also, you must use palm.

DJ: Do you recall any favorite times training with Yip Man?

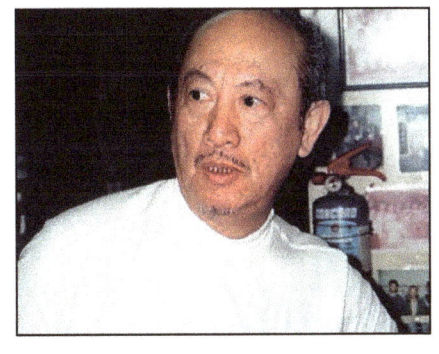

CCM: Usually in the morning I think I am clever. In the morning, not many students get up early, I go first. So now, I go to Sifu and he still not up yet. So I say, "Sifu, wake up, wake up, go to tea. After the tea, he say, "play the Siu Nim Tao." and I say, "Sifu, I am tired, I played many times already." He say, "OK, Chi Sao."

His Chi Sao is very very good. Excellent, you know? I remember once I say to Sifu, "Sifu, for example, Bong Sao to palm strike, I don't think it is useful." Then Sifu ask me if I had breakfast already. "Yes," I answered, "How long, one hour?" "No, two hours." he said, "OK, Chi Sao with me." He said you hit me, so I try to hit him very quickly. So, he hit me like this, very soft, I don't know where the power came from, or how come too quick, then I am against the wall!

DJ: So he used a short punch, or like a one inch punch?

[Grandmaster Chan retrieved his Batt Jom Dao swords and began demonstrating cutting techniques with the energy of a 30-year-old]

CCM: Yes, he gave me a short punch, but the punch I could see very clearly. It was very soft, just like Siu Nim Tao, but so powerful!

DJ: Why are there different Batt Jom Doa forms?

CCM: Everybody plays this differently partly because few of them learn before, maybe part learn later when Sifu was a little older, when his memory was not so good. Same thing with the wooden man. All of the fist forms he was able to keep track.

DJ: One of the difficult attributes in Chi Sao is to relax. Can you talk a little on this?

CCM: Actually, you must not be nervous. Some people think Chi Sao is fighting. But you have to make it relaxed. [Grandmaster Chan had me get up and he began to Chi Sao with me to make his point. He was very relaxed and agile, shifting and stepping to one side and then shooting out techniques] First, you don't be afraid to be hit by the people.

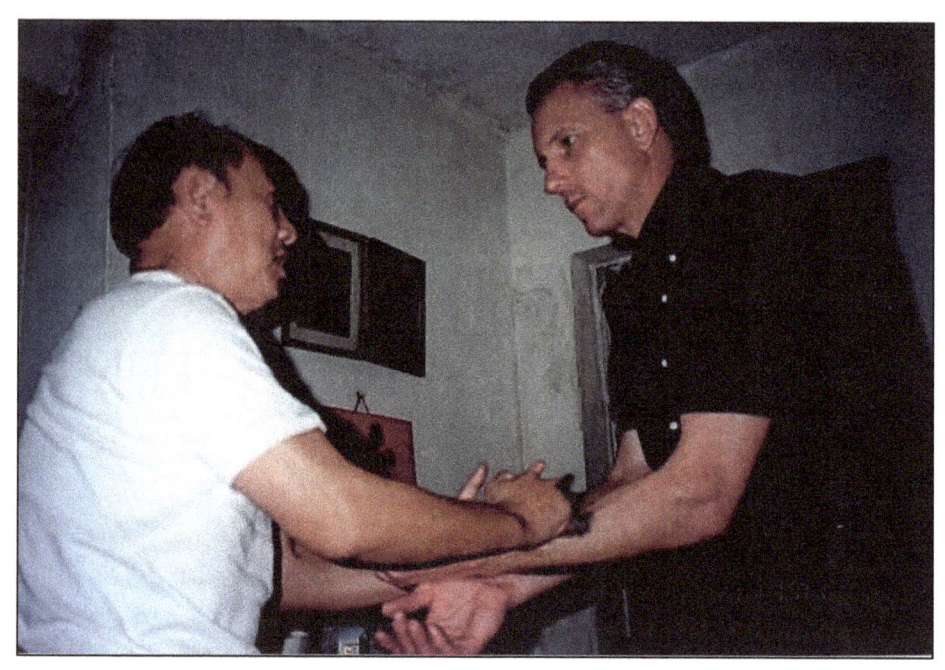

GM Chan demonstrating the double jut.

For you to Chi Sao with me oh, you are tall, I'm not afraid about you. You hit on me or nothing. Of course, if you are nervous, if you are nervous, you must win, you must win, then you must lose, you see? This is a part of being relaxed. Sifu always used to teach us, but nowadays, I say no more like that. Sifu would say, "Brothers Chi Sao, don't look to win or lose, it doesn't matter." Because he say, by the time you get to Chi Sao, you must always learn something, Pak Sao, Gong Sao.

If you are always like that in Chi Sao, you never have the chance to do this because the people let you do that. Even if you do it, maybe they not accept the success. But in Ving Tsun Chi Sao, maybe you can skip a few techniques, but when you deal with other styles, you have to use the striking techniques, because you have no chance, so if you don't hit them, you have no chance.

I remember long ago, we used to hit the other people, at that time, maybe we were too brave. Maybe not afraid of anything. So, you always win. How can I explain, when the distance close enough, you must attack, and you don't have to worry about your opponent's attacking you, because your attacking hands will be defense. Other people say, oh, Ving Tsun hands not very good looking, because when the enemy comes across, you fight straight on fiercely, side to side, punching, punching. So when other people see it, it's nothing. For example, tiger claw style, wow, really fancy, very good looking. But Ving Tsun hands, nothing fancy. But the thing you can see is the Bong Sao. But generally, there is no time for using a Bong Sao. So, if you don't relax, then you can lose your balance easy. When you are soft, you can trap easily. If your hands are too close and tense, they can be trapped. When I feel you lose your centerline, I take advantage. If you lose 5% of your centerline, I take 95% advantage. Also, don't demonstrate your techniques too quick.

Grandmaster Chan discussing form work.

DJ: Do you recall if Yip Man had any favorite techniques?

CCM: Well, he liked to get you to one side to hit. Also, if you lose your balance just a little, he would make you lose your balance big. He used his hands very free; you could not trap him.

DJ: You obviously still have very good soft pliable energy.

CCM: No, just when I was young, I did very hard work with Ving Tsun, but no, no more. But still in memory, you know? But sometimes memory is not good enough. My Sifu, I tell you, he look like this [Closes his eyes]. When I was young, I always try to trap him, it looks like he was sleeping, so I thought he sleeps. But always get hit by him. So, the next time, no way, no way, then he close his eyes, careful, careful. [We laughed] Sometimes he would use other stuff on us.

I remember sometimes he would use Ving Tsun to hit, sometimes he would use Choy Li Fut. Sometimes if you walk too close to him, he would hit you. This man is very funny, he will test you. Sometimes he was like a kid, he would like to play jokes on us.

DJ: Can you tell us a little about Chum Kiu?

CCM: Chum Kiu (Searching Bridge form) is same, to be relaxed, but one thing you must look at, you must be relaxed only at certain time. Don't be too relaxed. Kung Fu must have the Kung Fu spirit. For example, tiger claw has the tiger action. So, when you do the forms, you must imagine an enemy. You must be relaxed. So, in Chum Kiu, you must have the Ving Tsun spirit. For example, Siu Nim Tao is not always relaxed. The proper spirit must be in the movements.

Dinner with the Grandmasters and Masters L-R Steve Goericke, Chiu Hok Yin, Siu Yuk Men, Lee Wai Chi, Lee Moy Shan, Chow Tze Chuen, Donald Mak, Chan Chee Man, Wu Chun Nam, Author.

DJ: What do you feel the key to Ving Tsun is?

CCM: Suppose you punch me, then, Loy Lao Hoy Song, Luk Sao Chek Chung (When the hand comes, stay, when the hand leaves, follow) When the hand leaves after you catch it, you go forward. Make up your mind in an instant, don't think about hitting, just do it. Once you can hit, hit! And chase the body, don't chase the hands.

This is not easy. What do I mean? When both are close enough, I Ving Tsun, I want to hit. So if you are chasing the hands, you are not hitting the body. So you don't want to exchange with the hands, this is not fighting. You chase the body and hit; this is fighting. Don't chase the hands, if you can hit, hit. Don't think twice. Don't hesitate, if you hesitate, you lost a chance.

Also, when you face the opponent, you must be Doi Yang [Facing square]. This way, you can use both of your hands equally. Especially if I want to chase you to hit. Also, I always like to smile. Just to make you think I got nothing to do, you know? In Ving Tsun, the hands are very soft, the old man said, "The clever man doing the Ving Tsun must be clever." He said "That the one who ask him to learn Ving Tsun, and he is very huge and strong, but the one who is skinny, but smart, I teach him instead because he can use it." The other styles are different, they like them big and strong. Ving Tsun is different, you must use your mind.

DJ: Thank you, Grandmaster Chan.

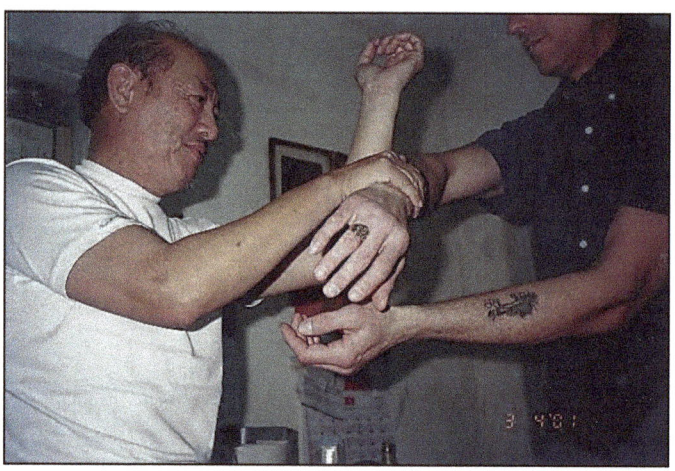

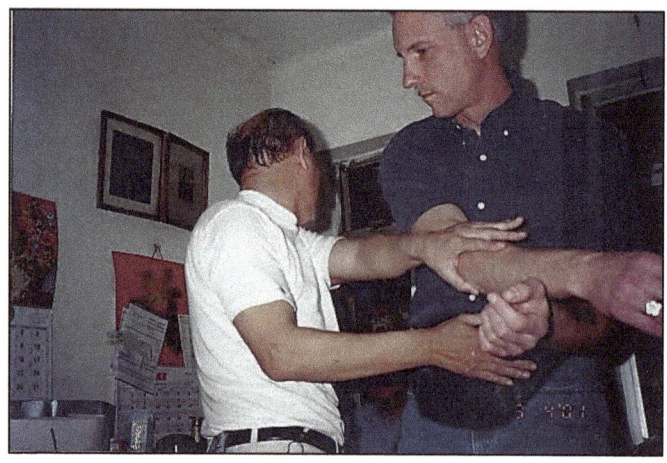

CHU SHONG TIN

Author with GM Chu at HK VTAA

DJ: Could you tell us how you got started in Ving Tsun?

CST: At first, when Yip Man started teaching at the Restaurant Workers Union, a few months later, I got a job as a bookkeeper there. I had weak health when I was young, so I was learning Tai Chi at night and slowly, slowly I began to compare the theories of Yip Mans Ving Tsun to Tai Chi, to see which is better being acceptable for me.

    I then make out the logic that Ving Tsun has better application than the Tai Chi I was learning so I signed up for classes with Yip Man and became a Disciple of Yip Man.

DJ: So you watched the classes?

CST: Yes, I watched the classes; I worked in the same premises as class. So, I listened to the theories, and slowly I began to compare Ving Tsun with Tai Chi.

GM Chu Shong Tin with Master Buick Yip at 1st Ving Tsun World Conference 1999.

DJ: How many people were in the class at the time when you enrolled?

CST: When Yip Man started the class, it was very difficult for him to introduce Ving Tsun. There was a group of about 20 or 30 people at the Restaurant Workers Union that started right away.

Yip Man was already teaching there for a few months before I got a job there. And then very slowly, people were separating from the classes, and by the time I joined, there were three of us left. Dai SiHing Leung Sheung, Lok Yiu, and I was the third one.

DJ: Do you recall in what year this was?

CST: 1951, I was 18 years old, first of January, 1951.

DJ: What were the differences in Ving Tsun that made you decide to learn it?

GM Chu demonstrating rooting power.

CST: To my understanding of Tai Chi at the time when I was learning it, the theory of Tai Chi is how to slide away oncoming force, and how to find the opponents weakness. You have to keep picking and picking for some time before you can find the opponents weakness, and then send an attack which means they are not in tract, or in one theory. The difference in Ving Tsun is that you have a whole set complete, one button contains everything. One key, a complete set of distinct, eh, solutions for the situation that you are at, the moment of contest. You don't have to wait for someone to come and attack you, and then do something. Or wait until they are out of guard to do something else. Ving Tsun is all in the condition you can apply it, the techniques. Whereas in Tai Chi, you have different techniques for different situations.

DJ: You are known as the King of Siu Nim Tao, how often do you practice this form?

CST: I do not have to practice the fist form anymore. I used to practice when I was younger in the morning before the class starts. Now, I don't have to practice the forms by the set, because throughout the process of giving instruction and demonstrating the forms, I am practicing.

DJ: Could you tell us in your opinion, what the essence of Siu Nim Tao is?

CST: Siu Nim Tao of course is the first fist form of Ving Tsun style, and it has all of the fundamental movements as you can see. And it can use the least strength if you do it right, you can apply a blocking technique without exerting strength at all. Which means if your opponent is exerting strength onto you, if you apply the technique right, or your body construction is correct, you can defend yourself by diminishing the oncoming force without exerting force of your own. This is number one. Number two, Siu Nim Tao can exert an internal force. Siu Nim Tao can train a concentration of the mind that can control your pulse and your blood flow in your body. Also, Siu Nim Tao is on one single spot, you never move one inch on your feet. The only attacking hands are one punch and the palm, all of the other movements are for defense.

But if the opponent were to come into your range, all you have to do is make a little change of the technique, and your defensive technique becomes an attacking technique.
Siu Nim Tao is inclusive of almost all of the attacking techniques that you need. Because the punch and the palm really is all you need if you can get them right, if you can get them through the opponents hands and into your opponent.

You don't need hooks, or low punches to hit your opponent. Once you get into the domain of your opponent's defense, it is easily like cutting bean curd. It is a piece of cake if you use the techniques of Siu Nim Tao correctly. [Grandmaster Chu showed me some photos, one being a demonstration he performed at the World Ving Tsun Conference in Hong Kong. GM Chu was standing on one leg while on a scale so as to measure the added weight while two large guys were attempting to push him over]

DJ: Is there a way to know if you are developing your Siu Nim Tao correctly, a feeling perhaps, or some way to recognize improvement?

Author with GM Chu Shong Tin, Mrs. Chu and two top female students.

CST: You cannot use whatever you improve on an opponent, because you will be seeing different opponents. Maybe one is stronger than you, maybe one is weaker than you. So you cannot evaluate your status of your level in Siu Nim Tao, but you can feel improvements by yourself if you do it right. Everyone has a different attitude, and a different way of mind or thinking. If you really work on Siu Nim Tao, you will be able to feel significant difference. In most cases, people only spend a short time on Siu Nim Tao. Maybe 90% of the people I see are not into Siu Nim Tao.

DJ: Does Siu Nim Tao have more influence in your Chi Sao than the other forms Chum Kiu and Biu Je?

CST: In the process of doing Chi Sao, because Siu Nim Tao is fixed and stable, but in Chi Sao you keep constantly moving. And once you are moving, it is not Siu Nim Tao. If you teach a guy only Siu Nim Tao, and go tell him to Chi Sao with a Sihing, he won't know how to move, because nobody ever taught him how to move. Eventually in Chi Sao, it is not just the techniques in Siu Nim Tao, but all the techniques, but these are even rooted from techniques in Siu Nim Tao.

DJ: When learning and practicing Chi Sao, which should one focus more on, offense or defense?

CST: I am more into finding out the theory of Ving Tsun and to apply the Ving Tsun in the Chi Sao. Most times when I Chi Sao with my older students at the school, I do not take offense, I take defense, I let the others attack me. And while I defend, I can apply the techniques according to the theory for defense. I never make hitting on my counterpart during the work out. But when I go out for contest, I have to take offense, and no one is ever able to block one of my movements.

If I want to punch, I get it in, if I want to palm, I will get the palm in. I had seven or eight contests before I opened my school and became a teacher. I never hurt my opponents fiercely, just give them red palm marks on their chest.

DJ: In the United States, Chinese tournaments have become very popular. In these tournaments they have Chi Sao competition. Would you comment on this?

CST: It's just like if you have a gun, and you go target practice, you don't have to think that one day I may have to shoot somebody. You just take this as training for your head, your hands, your eyes. You practice jogging, you don't have to go for competition. You just go for your own self reinforcement. Ving Tsun is just a method of training.

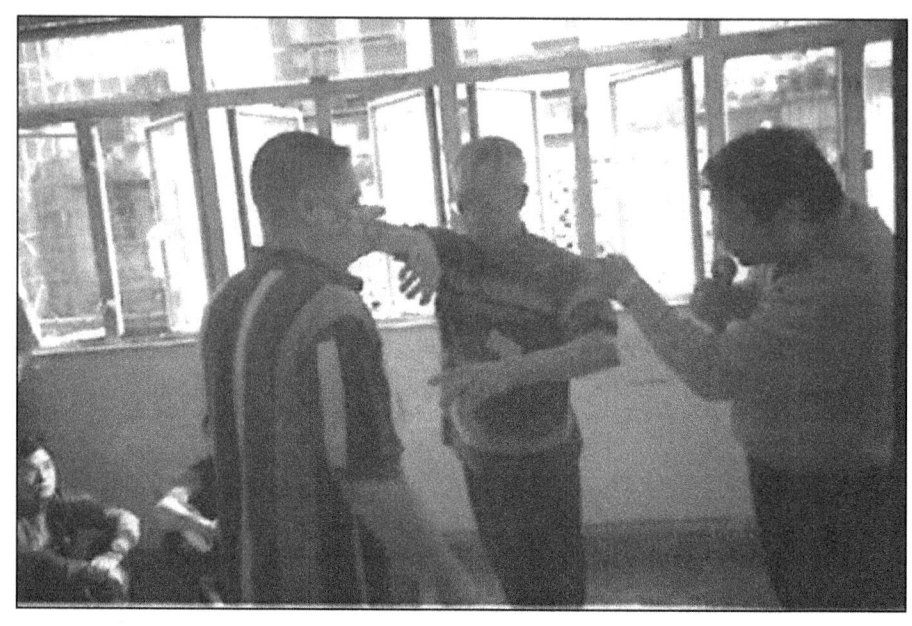

GM Chu explaining the finer points of bong.

DJ: In Chi Sao, do you have a favorite technique?

CST: No, nothing special, whatever I feel is appropriate.

DJ: Did you have a favorite person to Chi Sao with in class?

CST: I like variety; I do Chi Sao with everybody. By now, there is almost no one that I haven't Chi Sao with.

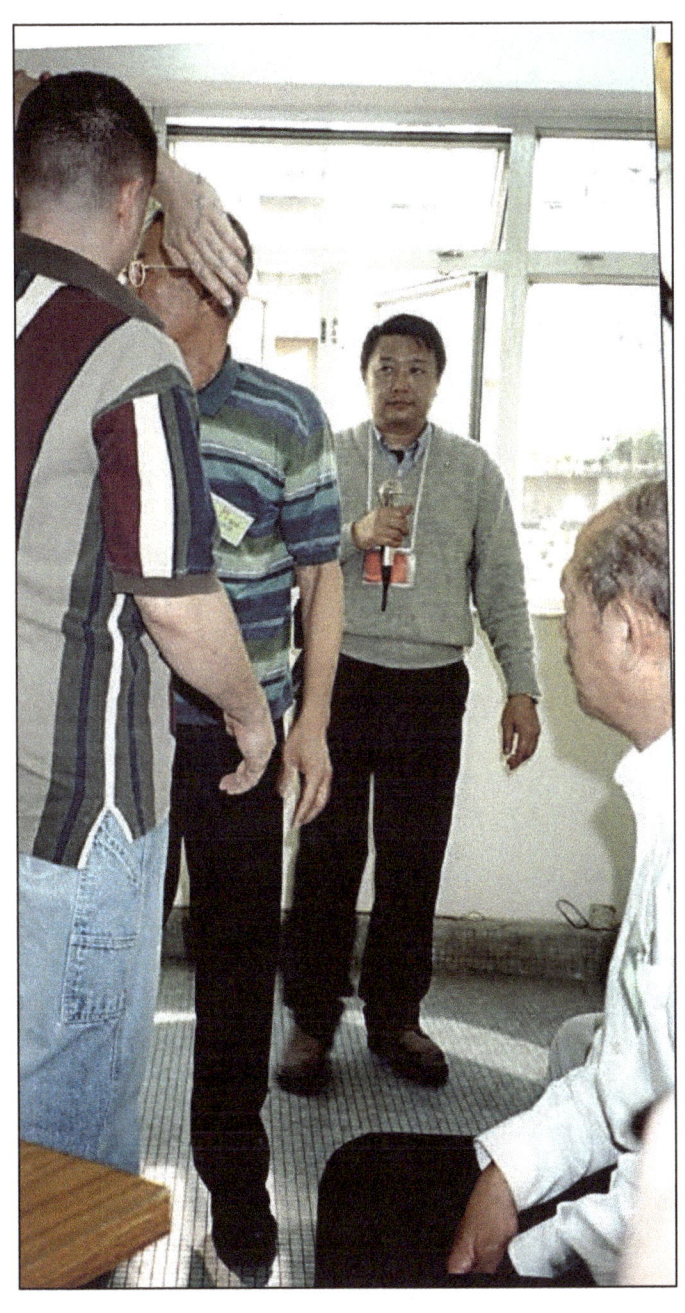

GM Chu using Brian McDonald to demonstrate a concept at the VTAA.

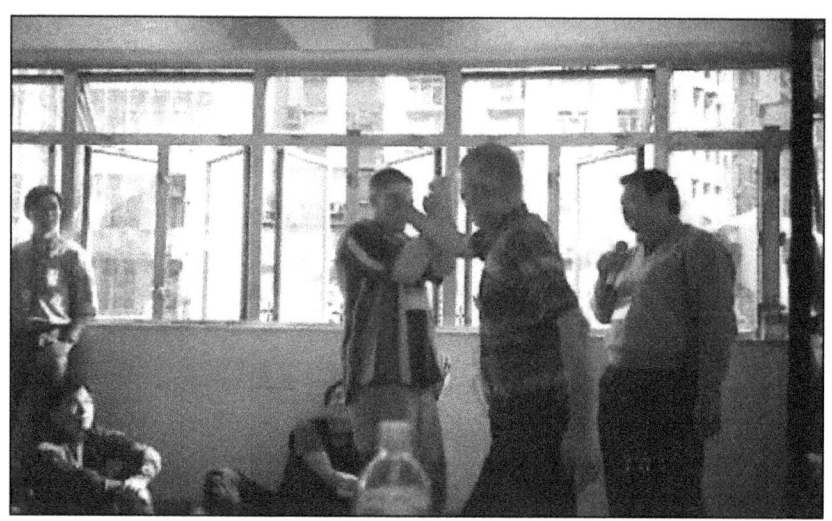

DJ: At the Ving Tsun Athletic Association last week, you were giving demonstrations on certain movements from Biu Je. Obviously, you are using your imagination to develop these demonstrations, can you talk about this?

CST: I do not have to formulate any particular demonstration. I can randomly give you a demonstration for any movement in the forms. If someone needs a demonstration, I can give you one right away.

Also, when I deal with other people from other styles, I can tell them that if they do their technique in this way, it will be more efficient. In Ving Tsun, every part of the body, the construction, configuration, has been so scientifically calculated to give the best function on each particular movement. A lot of people still don't understand this. They think all of these wild or large movements are very good. But actually, there is a basic requirement for the body's function in physical movement that you can exert good, efficient speed and strength.

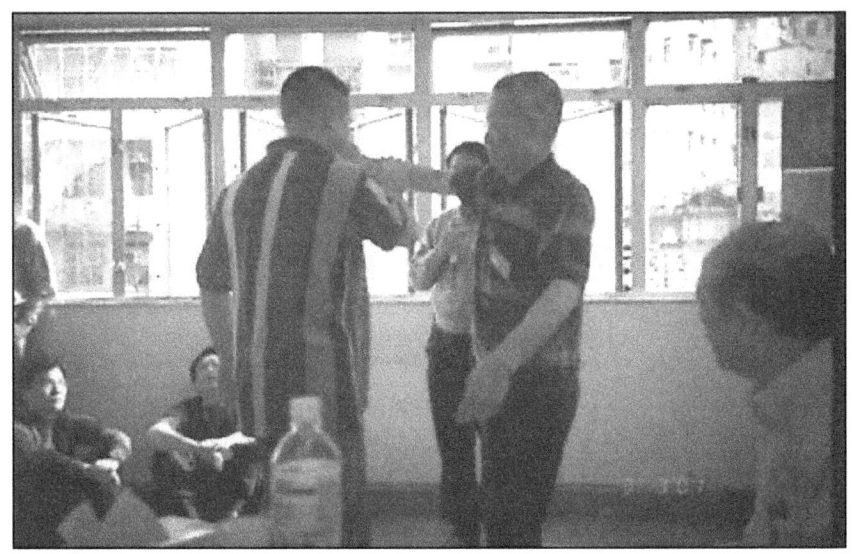

DJ: Some of the techniques from Biu Je (Shooting Fingers form) are considered for emergencies. Can you comment on this?

CST: It is not actually interpreted as for emergency case. Because once you use techniques from Siu Nim Tao and Chum Kiu, and in fact they are full, or you can apply all you learn in Siu Nim Tao and Chum Kiu fully, there is obviously no opportunity for your opponent to take you.

    Biu Je is just like a very powerful weapon. It really depends on if you want to apply it or not. It's like an arrow on full strength, whether you want to let go of your finger or not to give that striking force, which might not be necessary. So, it is not really for emergency purpose, it's just on the likelihood on whether you use or not.

DJ: When I first arrived to the Ving Tsun Athletic Association last week, you were giving a lecture where you used Brian to assist you. Do you do this all of the time at the VTAA?

CST: I started a tea party on the first Sunday of every month at the VTAA so that I could introduce my research and understanding. So, I conduct classes every month for the group on what my achievements are and pass it out. We all have a responsibility to the continued growth of Ving Tsun. [At the VTAA, several of the Grand Masters and second generation Sifu's hold class for their students. They have their own particular days and times to hold class. During the Tea Party GM Chu stated, all students from all schools and classes at the VTAA are welcome to participate]

DJ: Sir, I see that your class is beginning, before I go, I would like to ask one other question. Where do you see Ving Tsun now and in the future?

CST: Now first we talk about the future for Ving Tsun in the world of Martial Arts. Ving Tsun will keep on developing, will pass down from inheritance to inheritance, from generation through generation. There are two major main streams of Ving Tsun. Some people like to learn and explore Ving Tsun to the depth.
    Then there are those that like to promote it. Some people will close themselves behind the door, and do research work. Then there are the people out there selling it, pushing it. The people pushing it don't have to have much ability to push it, and the people pushing it don't have much knowledge of how it was made, they just know the name and try to sell it. But mostly, there are more salesman than researchers. That's OK, it is a good balance.

Thank you, GM Chu.

CHOW TZE CHUEN

L-R Donald Mak, GM Chow, Author

DJ: When did you become involved in Ving Tsun?

CTC: I started in 1955. From there, I never stopped learning Ving Tsun, from Siu Nim Tao, to Don Chi Sao (Single sticking hand) up to Chi Sao.

DJ: You were never shown Pak Sao (Slapping hand) or Lop Sao (grabbing hand)?

CTC: Yes, from Siu Nim Tao to don Chi Sao. I learned Siu Nim Tao for six months, and then after that don Chi Sao, and then rolling hands. There was no Pak, or Lop taught at that time.

DJ: Can you tell us why?

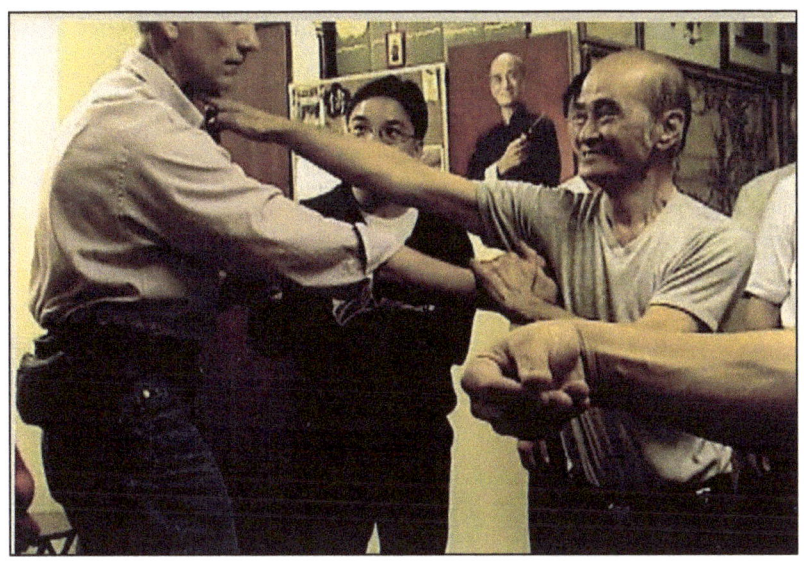

GM Chow demonstrating long arm techniques of Ving Tsun.

CTC: Yip Man Sifu taught differently to different people according to their level, how they commit, and how they learn. So, there was no fixed learning, or fixed curriculum to learn Pak

Sao, or Lop Sao, those other things, it all depends on the people. Yip Man asked me to demonstrate with him kicking techniques. So, I learned a lot from Yip Man about kicking because he had me do demonstrations.

[Master Donald Mak, a senior Disciple of GM Chow would serve as my interpreter. GM Chow was a very gracious man, with a spirit and energy that is very apparent for his age. At 76 years old, he demonstrated long arm techniques, as well as kicking techniques that really amazed me for his age. The speed at which GM Chow was able to move from one side to the other performing techniques was truly something to appreciate. The most interesting part of the demonstrations was when he showed me how he would deal with a tall long arm person as I. The techniques he performed were conducted with pin point accuracy. GM Chow would ask me to do a particular technique, which I would oblige but with respectful speed and energy, after all he is a GM and at the time 76 years old. But once he demonstrated his techniques, I was glad that I used restraint in my aggressive movements. Typically, the harder you attempt to hit someone in Ving Tsun the harder you are hit back, as your technique creates their technique. I was told later that not everyone when they visit are as mild as I was (just showing respect). That left me wondering what may have happened to those that tread here before I.]

DJ: So, some students got Pak Sao, Lop Sao, and others would get different things?

CTC: Yes, some students would be taught differently. Since I am same height as Yip Man, he liked to use me for kicking techniques. So, I would show foot work while Yip Man would go off and show other things. [GM Chow stands straight up from a sitting position on one leg, and begins to rotate his leg in a circle while it was chambered, and then does a few kicks from the chamber with terrific force].

According to Lok Yiu, he says, I only do straight punch and that's enough, I don't have to do much feet technique. But for me, the demand of Ving Tsun is that you are supposed to work your feet so that they are as flexible as your hands, which means that the hands and the feet are equal. Naturally the feet are more difficult to work on. What is the purpose of learning good kung fu, it's not just for self-defense, or beating up people? It's for self-development, and I just demonstrate this to you at my age. I am not trying to boost myself, but I just want to show you because you came all the way from Florida.

DJ: Do you teach Ving Tsun professionally?

CTC: I never teach Ving Tsun as a profession, maybe I am a half Sifu, [We all laughed]. I have my own day time job at the bus company that gives me support. But I started teaching Ving Tsun in 1962, but not as a profession because Yip Man Sifu always used to tell us that if you have a job that can support, that is enough. You do not rely on kung fu as a profession because if you teach as a profession, this means that your students are a client. So, if the relationship is dissatisfying, then sometimes you cannot teach equally. Maybe some students are lazy but they are rich, you cannot teach the good students equally. It is not fair. For example, traditionally to start learning the dummy form, we give a red pocket. Even some other Sifu's they might charge $100 (HKD) per movement on the dummy. So maybe they put in a few more movements.

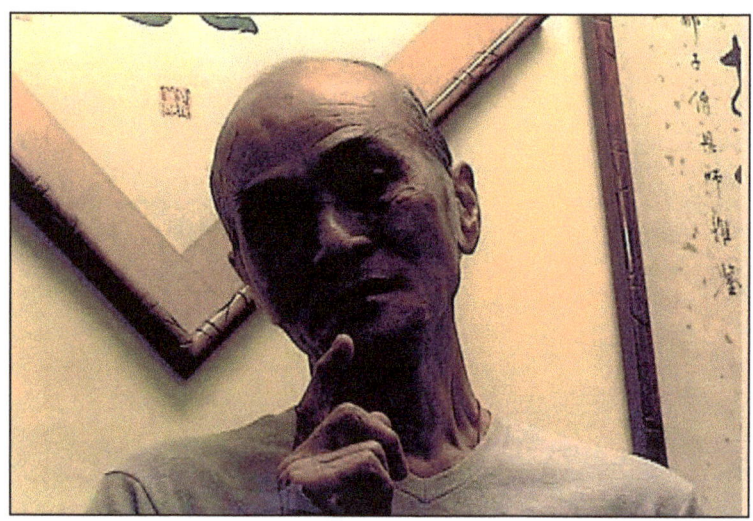

DJ: Movements or section?

CTC: Yes, movements. Let's look at the Batt Jom Doa (Eight Chopping Way Knives), not many people learned Batt Jom Doa directly from Yip Man Sifu. Myself, Chu Shong Tin, and a couple of others. At the time during Chinese New Year, Koo Sang came to visit Yip Man Sifu. So, I came to visit and Koo Sang answered the door and said that Yip Man Sifu was not here. But Yip Man Sifu heard my name and asked me to come in and sit down. After a while, Yip Man Sifu asked Koo Sang to leave first, and then he asked me to do the whole dummy form for him.

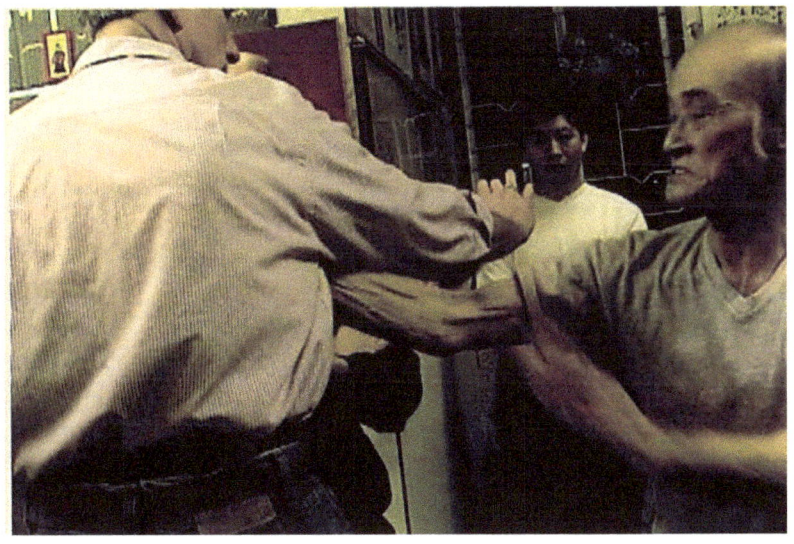

DJ: Do you recall what year this was in?

CTC: Yes, it was in the late 60's.

DJ: What does training in Chi Gerk consist of?

CTC: Our way of Chi Gerk is not with holding of the hands. We start using one leg and we must balance the body. All the techniques are Bong Gerk, Tan Gerk, and Fuk Gerk.

DJ: Do you recall who the most aggressive Chi Sao player was in class?

CTC: Wong Shung Leung, no doubt about that. When I was an assistant instructor for Yip Man Sifu, I came across many kinds of hands, many kinds of energy, with different people. At the time, myself and a couple of others used to take care of the class.

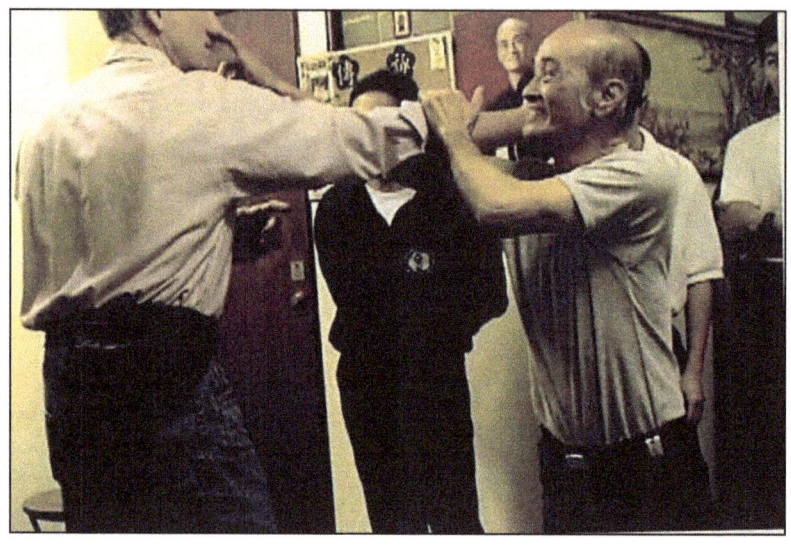

DJ: Can you mention what the strong point of Ving Tsun is in your opinion?

CTC: Now I think Ving Tsun is more technical or is more useful to attack while you are withdrawing. So if someone is attacking you, you can attack while backing up. Yip Man Sifu said that if you can learn retreat and attack, this is more difficult, more technical, but good. So, Ving Tsun is very good for attacking while withdrawing, so, retreat and attack.

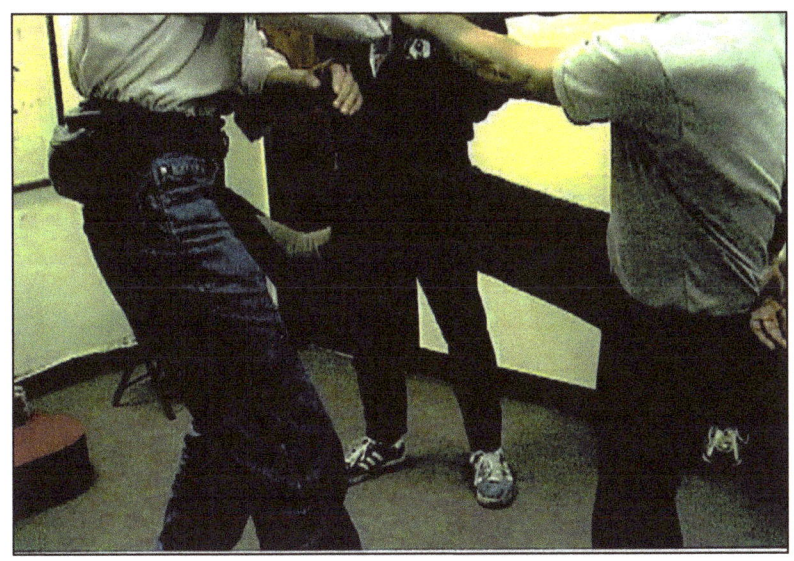

Also, the long bridge. Everyone says that Ving Tsun is short bridge, but it has very good long bridge work too. Although I am shorter, I can do long bridge to defend. [GM Chow asks me to stand up and to throw a punch at him. So, I throw a punch at him and all of a sudden, my arm is smacked away and he is not in front of me, but to the side of me with his two fingers pressed into my throat. This all happened in a blink of the eye. He has me throw another punch and now he is on the opposite side with his hand pressed into my side.

This was truly a learning experience. GM Chow was so quick and agile, but yet was quite capable of controlling his strikes. He also demonstrated inch punch power on Brian sending him flying]

DJ: Can you explain more on kicking techniques?

CTC: Because you are tall or thick, it is difficult to defend against these kicking techniques. Please stand up and I will demonstrate. [He asks me to throw a punch, and all of a sudden, my arm is deflected as he moves to the side and my knee is collapsed and his fingers have stopped just short of my eyes. When I refocused from his fingers to his face, he was smiling with a big grin looking at me amused] You have to be at a high level to do demonstrations at this level. Not everyone is as mild as you, so you must always be able to perform these techniques.

DJ: When you were learning Chi Sao, were there any formal Chi Sao techniques taught?

CTC: No fixed curriculum, as I said before, according to your level, and then just doing your techniques, one or two movements. No Tan Da, Lop Da, was taught consistently like that. Just bring out one or two techniques.

DJ: So, Yip Man didn't have a formalized method of teaching techniques in Chi Sao either?

CTC: That's right, he taught you according to your ability, so there was no fixed teaching method.

DJ: Is your sensitivity developed to a point where you don't have to worry about your centerline anymore?

CTC: Please stand up, I will show you. [He has me throw several various techniques directed towards his centerline. He moves very slightly without any effort, and simultaneously attacks my soft areas, eyes, groin, throat] Also, don't chase the hands, chase the body. Chasing the hands is no good. At the advanced levels, you don't need to worry about the centerline.
But in the beginning, you first must learn to protect the centerline.

DJ: In your opinion sir, what do you feel is the essence of Ving Tsun?

CTC: In my opinion, the essence of Ving Tsun lies in inch power, footwork, and kicking techniques, especially good techniques. The legs must be as flexible as the hands. There is no perfect superman, everybody will have a chance to be defeated. Bear in mind that there is no limitation to learning. Learning has no limitations, never be ignorant, never think that you are perfect, you learn and you teach.

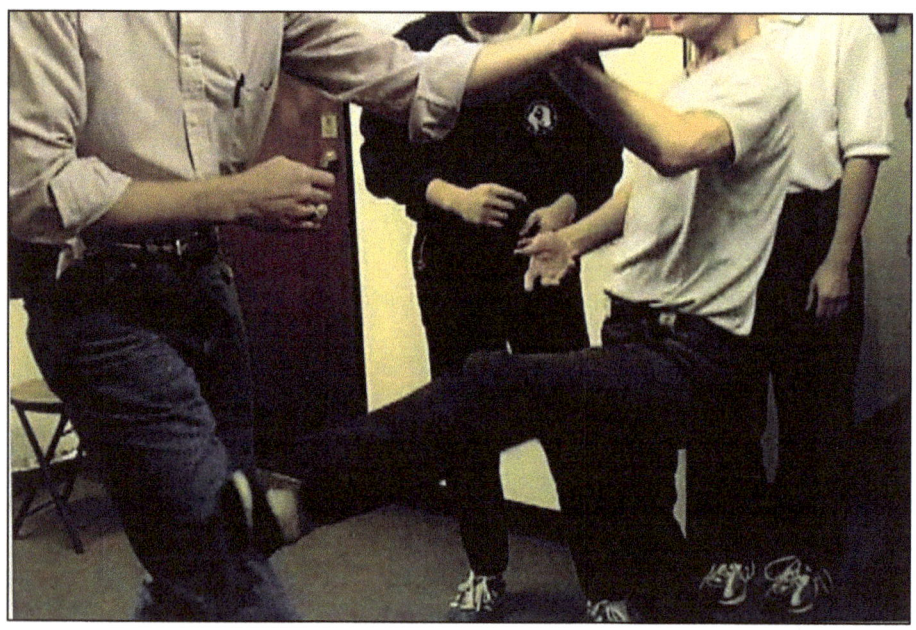

DJ: I have taken up enough of your time, I have one more question if you don't mind sir?

CTC: Please.

DJ: Is there any advice that you could impart on the best way to develop your Ving Tsun?

CTC: It is difficult to give any advice. But for people to have good Ving Tsun, and to put it into you, to develop it into yourself, first, you must like Ving Tsun. It is difficult though if you are lazy. But my example to you is me, being an old guy at 76 years old, I still can kick, still can Chi Sao, and I am still healthy because of my Ving Tsun. I still practice all of the time, I never stop.

DJ: Thank you Grandmaster Chow.

SIU YUK MEN

Grandmaster Siu Yuk Men with Author at the VTAA.

DJ: Can you talk a little about Yip Man?

SYM: Sifu Yip Man was a very educated man. His family in Foshan was a very good family. He came to Hong Kong during the revolution. He said that with Ving Tsun you must use your brain. Yip Man was very clever. I can tell you a true story. At that time, he could also do some Dit Da medicine, and I introduced a friend to him for treatment.

He was very nervous about the acupuncture and that maybe he would die. He asked Yip Man Sifu, "Oh, will the acupuncture hurt?" What do you think Yip Man said? "Oh, you are lucky, if you were hit a little bit more to this side, you would have died immediately.

But with this you are lucky, you don't need acupuncture." And then he put some Dit Da Jow on him and he asked him he if he was all better now. My friend said oh yes, thank you. He was very happy. So you see, Yip Man Sifu was very clever.

DJ: So, he would build up the injury and then let him down easy for his relief?

SYM: Of course.

DJ: What was training like with Grand Master Yip Man?

SYM: During that time, eh, Sifu not teaches very fast, because you must practice good. He mentioned to me that you must be correct. When you do all the movements, they must be correct and your stance, and then you do more and more of the same before he teach you more. When Yip Man came to Hong Kong, people didn't know Ving Tsun techniques, they see Tan Sao (Dispersing hand), Fuk Sao (Retaining hand) slowly, it is not good looking. So, people ask themselves, this is fighting techniques? It looks stupid!

But when you do it more and more, and then you are thinking why? Why do this, and why do this? Why you can do this and somebody else cannot. It all originates from the brain. When you do everything correct, even if you do it quick, my brain will always refer to the correct position. You can see that when you do the Siu Nim Tao, you do every movement slowly, and correctly. You can feel it is very easy, light, without any support. So that if you do not do it correct, you will realize it.

DJ: When did you begin teaching Ving Tsun?

SYM: I have a good job with the Government, so I began teaching only a few years ago, because when I retire, I will have something to do. Even Wong Shun Leung and Yip Ching ask me why are you not teaching? But I have been teaching my friends son and a few others privately.

DJ: So, from the time Grand Master Yip Man passed away until just a few years ago, you didn't teach Ving Tsun?

SYM: Since the Masters passing, I practice with Yip Ching, and eh, even Yip Ching not teaching, so we practice together and some other classmates, so that we keep some of Yip Man students together, such as Chan Chee Man, even Wong Shun Leung. We come up here to VTAA to practice. The most important part of Ving Tsun practice is Chi Sao, so we practice a lot of this. So that after all of these years we continue, so that our minds can be free. Recently I write an article, "50 Year Legacy." Also, I write about Chum Kiu, I also mention Chi Sao. You should be able to do Chi Sao without any thinking.

DJ: Does this apply to forms practice as well?

SYM: Yeah, of course, but in the beginning you must do thinking. Why Master Yip Man tell us everybody who practice Ving Tsun becomes a clever man? Because to learn Ving Tsun you must always use your brain, you are always thinking, whether it is technical or logical, you know? You do this, of course you must think so that you can improve yourself. Even when I am teaching, I find this is why I can't do something. So that even in Chi Sao, you find things out suddenly.

Suppose somebody is teaching another format in Ving Tsun, I don't argue format. Now, there are many people teaching, and I don't know whether it is Yip Man style, but some are not teaching Chi Sao, teaching Ving Tsun without Chi Sao! Maybe a little Chi Sao, they say Chi Sao is no use. When fighting you touch together, but they don't realize that Chi Sao teach you to react properly.

Even if I don't know kung fu and you attack me, I will defend myself. This is human being reaction, even when you don't know kung fu. If I punch you, you must try and stop the punch, or I will knock you back. So, Chi Sao teach you to defend and attack correctly. Because now Ving Tsun is very famous, and that also many other Ving Tsun styles come up, and even Yip Man said Ving Tsun is only half so that maybe somebody can upgrade himself.

DJ: What do you mean by half?

SYM: I think he means that Ving Tsun is a whole set, he said Ving Tsun you can only learn half, and still some not learn it all. I think you heard something about this. [Someone can only really understand about half of all that Ving Tsun is] There are maybe 20 different styles of Ving Tsun, some have Chi Sao, some say they find no use for it. I have a student that learn Ving Tsun from somewhere else, he even said that Chi Sao is of no use.

DJ: Are your teaching methods the same as Grand Master Yip Man?

SYM: Yes. Sifu teach step at a time. You get up to a level, and then you learn a new level. If you are not up to a level, and you are taught very quickly, of course you can do it, but later your success not very good. But step by step, then you can catch the idea, and handle it very well. It is like education in writing Chinese characters, with a brush. If you are quick, then it is not beautiful, but one step at a time, you will become very good, and by the time you are 70 years old, and you pick up a brush and do it, it will be very good because you are hard working at it.

Grandmasters L-R: Lee Wai Chi, Siu Yuk Men, Chan Chee Man at the VTAA.

It's your reward for hard working. Of course, in the beginning you know how to write, but you don't know how to do it beautiful, you see?

DJ: You refer to correct position, can you talk about this?

SYM: OK, so maybe you are upset by others in Ving Tsun, you can see in Ving Tsun if your position is correct to determine why I always keep my position correct and not let you affect my position. Maybe you are a tall one, or a short one, but I must always keep my position correct. Suppose you throw a punch, and I use a Bong Sao (Wing hand). Now since you are tall, maybe I won't use a Bong Sao because the position may not be correct for that. You must use correct position. You must learn to use the techniques, and train to release them from your body. You must use proper structure and let the position do the work. If your position not correct, I will hit you easy. So regardless of how tall or short you are, your position must always be correct and relative.

Sifu told me that if you fight somebody, you go ahead and punch them two and three times, if you cannot hit them, keep back and let your enemy attack you. And if you cannot defend yourself, you better get out of there. This is why I like Ving Tsun, it makes sense, it is straight to the point.

DJ: What about the Ving Tsun Punch, would you care to elaborate?

SYM: When I punch you, and you go back, you must release your energy forward. If you do not continue forward with your punch, the punch will come back into you, so continue forward with the punch. In Ving Tsun, where does your power come from?

DJ: I suppose some would say from the ground, through the hips and shoulders and through the arm to the fist.

SYM: WHY? Suppose somebody cannot control their punch, because it means the brain does not have that command, and then they don't know where the working power is from. And then suppose I punch, my force continues. But if I hit someone, there is resistance, so you must continue through. It is very difficult to define. Actually, the power comes from the brain, also from your training. If your training has been good, then your brain will remember. In emergency, your brain will have a tendency to forget all things. But if you always practice good, even during emergency, your brain, and your movements will come to you, because what you do before is very correct. I think you can catch my meaning.

In Loy Lao Hoy Song, Luk Sao Chek Chung (When the hand comes stay, when the hand leaves follow) this is also from the brain. Of course, just as well as your reaction, your feeling, and the sudden changes in balancing. All of this comes from the brain. Getting back to Grand Master Yip Man, some students may tell him, "you teach me too slow." So, Yip Man say, "If you are not patient, and if you do not like your brain to think, you will not learn good techniques of Ving Tsun," the Master said.

You must have patience, you must think, and he said every Ving Tsun guy will become a clever man. You learn Ving Tsun, and you will become a clever man because you always use your brain to think. If not, then you cannot learn good techniques of Ving Tsun.

DJ: Would you explain the power of Ving Tsun techniques?

SYM: I think you know about the techniques learned by Yip Man. Sifu told me that it is from a woman. Why a woman cannot use other styles? Other styles are for men, so that it use a lot of power and energy. Why Ving Tsun can slowly pitch and then apply the power. Of course, if your training is good, you can apply the point of power. Why the other styles are not very easy to apply power, because the muscles are so tight. If you do not relax, how can you apply the power? I teach a student that did another style for 20 years. So, I advise him to not do Ving Tsun anymore. He always add what he did before. Because Ving Tsun is quite different you see, very different from other styles. Why Sifu tell us, "If you study Ving Tsun don't make your muscles big." Although your muscles look very powerful, when you attack, the point of power will not be very good. In Ving Tsun we use explosion power. Of course, Bruce Lee learned beautiful inch power.

Ving Tsun you see must be relaxed. So big muscles mean it becomes more of a push. It must be an explosion, so you must be relaxed with correct position to do this. [At this point, GM Men demonstrates by punching my hand while he is seated, I noted the difference between a tight muscle punch, and one that explodes while delivered in a relaxed state. All I can say is that it was very obvious indeed.] So, you see, even if I am sitting down here, I can still use the power because of being relaxed and by using my brain. I'm relaxed when I punch, it has more explosive power. I use less energy as well you see, so when you meet the punch power, you will be hurt inside.

Even though I am sitting down, I cannot use the ground. I only can use this [Holds up his fist] and this, [Points to his head]. Of course, when fighting, the ground supports me to add more power, but it all comes from the mind. I make all of the working power focus in my attack. Very simple. But how to use it? Suppose you cannot get in contact with the mind, it freezes up, your muscles get stiff. So, you must learn to relax. So even with a kick, If I kick you, I remain standing in same spot. Even a big guy 200 pounds, I kick him, he will go back and my step still remain in position. Why? Because when I kick him, I use my working power. If I punch you the point of power is here? [Points to the three lower knuckles on his fist] How can you make the power to get there? Of course, you train, you must make your foundation good.

DJ: How can you relate this in terms of Chi Sao?

SYM: Suppose you are rolling hands slowly with good stance and then you will always be in good position. But of course, some people have no patience doing this, and they go very quick because they want Gong Sao (Talking hands) and this makes them very happy. In rolling hands, if I am in good position [He has me stand up and he demonstrates his Bong Sao against my Fuk Sao] you cannot affect me, but I can affect you. In good position, I diminish your power. In good position, you can feel the power. The power you feel it is your power, not my power, because I use my position against your power. My position borrows your power and turns it around to you. But as soon as you are not in good position, your power then becomes powerful. This is what Yip Man Sifu used to do. He simply use your forward power with his position. He would make you lose your balance very easily because of this, and he would beat you easily.

So, it is a training method, not only talking. Talking is no use, you know the meaning, yes this is clever, but if you not practice it well, you will not learn to make it practical. So you must be hard working and to train correct.

Do you know Chinese? You can see, when Yip Man Sifu named his two sons Yip Ching and Yip Chun, Chun means correct, Ching also means correct. Ching is also perfect, or accurate, in Chinese, Chun, Ching is quite similar. I believe that he used the names of his 2 sons, it came from Ving Tsun. So that he wants his two sons correct, Chun Ching, therefore it is good. Of course, this is only my feeling, I never asked Sifu about this.

DJ: So, you think Yip Man gave his sons their name because of Ving Tsun?

SYM: I admit that this is what I find, I think he did name his sons because of Ving Tsun, it is very clever.

DJ: What stands out in your mind in regard to Yip Man's instruction and what was his emphasis in learning?

SYM: We were lucky that Yip Man Sifu would help us learn with his demonstrations. But then he would make us use thinking. You must use your mind, look at it that way, and look at it this way, always thinking and looking at it. When you learn with all of the thinking, then your mind can pick it out when necessary. Let's say I meet a guy that I am not familiar with, his movement, his force, it will always be different. It cannot only be one way, every situation is different. So, you use your position in certain ways, and your force must be based on your stance, otherwise, you will have no power. Each position has a certain range it should be used in, and your stance will affect this for each different situation.

DJ: Is there any particular training that you do after so many years of practicing Ving Tsun?

SYM: Every morning I do Siu Nim Tao for one hour. I still train all of the forms every day because I am teaching, I want to keep the good technical ability for my students. Also to do more thinking, do more training, and then make it easier to get. Training your body and your mind will make it easier to get answers.

DJ: Do you recall any advice Yip Man would give relative to fighting?

SYM: Yip Man Sifu said don't be afraid of being beat, if you are afraid, then you will be beat by others. You must have confidence and then good position, and of course they cannot get in. Of course, if I cannot punch you or get into your defense, I will go away. You have energy to run away for saving yourself. Yip Man Sifu also said, even though your theory of technique is of good understanding, but the student has no patience to learn, and not hard working, not training hard, not take care of good position, not take care of all of the foundation, then the success is less, it will be much less.

Ving Tsun luncheon L-R: Chiu Hok Yin, Siu Yuk Men, Chu Shong Tin, Lee Moy Shan, Chow Tze Chuen, Donald Mak.

DJ: What was Bruce Lee like in training?

SYM: Bruce Lee, when we trained together, of course he only learned for a couple of years, and then he left from Hong Kong to America for education. Also, he was clever, and hard working. If he not training so good, his success not so good. I had received a letter about Jeet Kune Do, Bruce Lee's JKD. He said something very interesting, he said that Ving Tsun is its mother, JKD is the son, so if you want JKD good, it means JKD must have mothers' milk. He is very good, eh? He said, "If you want JKD good, it must have Ving Tsun because if it does not have milk, maybe they not grow up good." He was very clever.

DJ: What do you miss the most about training in the early days of Ving Tsun in Hong Kong?

SYM: Of course, Yip Man Sifu teaching us! He used to teach us very conventionally. He advised us not to get big, so that you can increase the speed which increases the power. So if you do this method, it is better. He would start us slowly, six months and still on Siu Nim Tao. Chan Chee Man start very slowly, few months, and maybe just single stick hand. So that during this time you make your foundation good. You must be very consistent. The theory of Ving Tsun is accuracy, Chun and Ching is correct, accurate, always use your brain.

Suppose you never use your brain, then you can't get in. So, you must do a lot of calculating, day and night. For example, if all human beings use nothing but the computer to do math, later, you won't know how to do it without one. So, you must have foundation. That is why Master Yip Man teach us very slowly, and this is why you must have patience. Nowadays most young men are not patient. If you teach them for a few months and it is still Siu Nim Tao, then they will go away. They cannot stand the patience.

DJ: Can you comment on Siu Nim Tao?

SYM: Siu Nim Tao looks very easy, but if you do it with accuracy, then it is very difficult, not very easy. Some students after one year, still cannot get it. Yip Man Sifu said that if you do it with a very easy time, and you spent the time on it, if you do it very right, then you do it very easy. You force your stance to support you, and then you make it very easy.

DJ: Do you have any advice for future Ving Tsun generations?

SYM: Even now I try and get more and more of Ving Tsun. This is automatic from how I used to practice before. You must always work on your foundation to develop your working power. So even today, I still train all of my foundation, and always think to find answers in Ving Tsun, OK?

Thank you, Grandmaster Siu.

WU CHUN NAM

Author with Master Wu Chun Nam

DJ: What made you decide on learning Ving Tsun Kung fu and who was your Sifu?

WCN: Wong Shun Leung, he was my High School classmate as well, we are the same age. Wong Shun Leung asked me if I wanted to learn Ving Tsun and I said no. I never heard of Ving Tsun Kung Fu, so I didn't want to learn it. About 6 months later, Wong Shun Leung had his first contest with a southern Praying Mantis guy, and he asked me if I wanted to go with him to watch the contest. We were two high school kids at the time and when I see the contest, I did not see Wong Shun Leung beating up the guy. I practically could not see the movements of his hands, but the opponent was bleeding all over the place.

Then I really admired Ving Tsun and I said to Wong Shun Leung, "yes, I want to learn Ving Tsun!" But I had to stop my training for a little while and continue with high school. I continued again in 1959 with Ving Tsun. At that time, we practiced very intensely and have a lot of actions.

DJ: Did you have contests as well?

WCN: My first contest with outside style was in 1961 and the contestant was a northern style, and the contest only last for 50 seconds. There even was a movie recording made of the fight. And then I send the film over to Bruce Lee when Bruce asked to watch it. The movie film has been gone ever since.

DJ: Did you know Bruce Lee very well?

WCN: I practiced a lot with Bruce Lee because in 1958 when Bruce learned from Yip Man, obviously, Yip Man was getting old, and did little Chi Sao with Bruce. And actually, Bruce would go to Wong Shun Leung's place a lot of times to practice with us. Wong Shun Leung would practice Chi Sao with Bruce and he is the one that taught Bruce the Ving Tsun aspects.

DJ: What was your opinion of Bruce Lee's Chi Sao at the time?

WCN: He was not really that good when he started. He was sloppy with his techniques. He was not good with the techniques of the Ving Tsun movements, and inside skills with the techniques. But Bruce Lee was very devoted and he was very hard-working person. So, he has achievements afterwards. When Bruce Lee goes to school at Xavier, he used to live right down the road from here. After school, Bruce with his school bag on his back, he would throw punches in the air on his way home when he was walking.

DJ: Your method of teaching Ving Tsun, is it the same after all of these years as the Wong Shun Leung method?

WCN: My teaching through all of these years is still the same as the way I learned it from Wong Shun Leung.

DJ: Did you ever meet Yip Man, or practice in any of his classes?

WCN: I just visit the school of Sigung, but I seldom would participate in the class.

DJ: Can you talk a little about the Ving Tsun forms?

WCN: I consider Siu Nim Tao and Chum Kiu being the most necessary in representing the martial art of Ving Tsun, and Biu Je is like an additional extension of the first two sets. As you know, Siu Nim Tao is like the base, like the a, b, c, alphabet of Ving Tsun. And Chum Kiu gives all the opportunity to extend contact with your opponent, and Biu Je is needed when it comes to crises and extra destruction. If you are talking about the essence of Ving Tsun the first two sets are very useful. If you try to learn Biu Je before your first 2 sets are good, or your base foundation is not good with the first two sets, the destruction capability of Biu Je could come back to you if you use instead of your opponent if you use Biu Je.

If your first two sets foundation is not enough, and you try to use Biu Je, your body's speed and strength, the adhesiveness of your body's construction, the movements you try to make to destroy your opponent, will eventually come back to you, especially with the twisting of your arm movements in Biu Je. So you see, these movements in Biu Je are very dangerous to the one who practice it because you take a very big chance with movements like this. [Master Wu demonstrates by dropping his elbow down in front of him with his wrist tucked in towards his chest] What if you don't have proper base, you will just get stuck. I don't know if you guys practice long reach, but if your long reach is not good enough, you can get confined by your opponent. We practice long bridge; you can lift the weight of your opponent with this.

DJ: During the time when you were training, did you practice Chi Gerk (Sticking legs)?

L-R Author, Wu Chun Nam, Chan Chee Man, Buick Yip

WCN: No. We didn't practice that much Chi Gerk. As a matter of fact, I don't teach that much to my students because I did not specialize in it. Just a few basic techniques.

L-R Wu Chun Nam, Chan Chee Man, Chow Tze Chuen, Andrew Ma, Author, Brian McDonald at the VTAA.

DJ: When you fought in the contests, did you have any favorite techniques?

WCN: I seldom use Bong Sao in contest. I would mostly use the Pak Sao, even for kicks. But mostly what I memorize, I would use very efficiently, I would gong and then Dai Jeurng, something like a Po Pai Jeurng (Butterfly palms) when opponent would kick, and I would knock him off his feet and he would fly way back.

DJ: How many Gong Sao contests did you have?

WCN: Only one, and that one was filmed which is the film I gave to Bruce Lee. The reason why is because Wong Shun Leung had done too many fights and beat everybody up, and there was nobody left for us. People back in those days worked out very hard because there are always opportunities, and you don't want to lose if the opportunity comes to you. So maybe you wake up tomorrow, and somebody would challenge you. Wong Shun Leung had the most fights. He even started fights to let others finish them off. Later on, a lot of styles when they hear you are form Ving Tsun, they then don't bother, no problem. Have you heard of Wong Kiu? He was a praying mantis instructor and he had plenty of students. He would conduct fights between Mantis and Ving Tsun and they lose all the time. Then Wong Kiu changed his mind and learned Ving Tsun. Hung Gar had very few fights.

DJ: What do you miss the most about the early days of training in Ving Tsun?

WCN: 1959-1962 we used to practice for hours at a time, even Saturdays and Sundays as well as throughout the week.

DJ: I don't want to take up much more of your time away from your students, but could you give any advice for future Ving Tsun students?

WCN: Well, most people use sneakers when they practice Ving Tsun instead of Kung Fu shoes [With cloth bottoms] and so the ones who wear sneakers their stance is much wider in Siu Nim Tao. You see the Siu Nim Tao stance is so close, and you see this guy standing with his stance so wide? You must concentrate on a good stance.

The very basic thing is that you cannot stand as wide as you want in Siu Nim Tao because when you get to Chum Kiu you have to shift and if your stance is too wide, and you shift, the leg in the rear stance you can commit, but what about your front leg? You lose the essence of the shifting technique in Chum Kiu. I have seen this allot even in Hong Kong too. You see, the sneakers grab the floor easier. The Kung Fu shoes are more slippery, they force you to grab the floor. So, the sneakers grab for you and make you lazy, or not concentrate on the stance. You really have to work on your stance and feet.

L-R Donald Mak, Chan Chee Man, Wu Chun Nam, Lee Wai Chi

You are supposed to be able to lift your feet right after you shift. Make sure your feet are not too wide. When you train good on your feet, your feet are always ready for action because you have concentration on your feet, so if you use slippery shoes you will always concentrate on it. Now if you use sneakers, you do not train your feet. So, you are only doing more or less the same thing, but you are not training the feet, so your feet are not flexible.

If you want to kick, you have to think, but if you are training the feet at the same time as the top, anytime you shift, anytime you want to kick, it's ready because you are on guard because every second you are concentrating. It's always perpetual training, you train the top, you train the bottom simultaneously. It's not just to look good, but do you have any strength in your stance? So, in Chi Gerk, some people try it, but they don't have the stance, so it is no good. They perform the Chi Gerk, but there is no Kung Fu in it. So, although I don't know much about Chi Gerk, I always practice one leg Siu Nim Tao and so the stance is very strong. So, you must work on your stance, you must concentrate on this, OK?

Thank you Master Wu.

CLIFF AU YEUNG

School Pamphlet of Master Cliff Au Yeung

DJ: Was Wong Shun Leung still going out for Gong Sao competition when you first joined his school?

CAY: When I learned Kung Fu with Master Wong at that time, he had stopped taking competition from the outside. I started in 81', he fought from the 50's to the end of the 60's, in the 70's he totally stopped so that he could teach full time. But one time at a seminar maybe 90 or 92, we were in Europe for a seminar, I was with him as his interpreter. So, we landed in England and when we stepped off the plane, the instructor comes up to us and says that this guy challenged two of his assistants, and that he knew he was going to be at the seminar. Master Wong said, "OK, he is welcome." So, at the seminar after the speech, Master Wong had a habit of always asking "if anyone would like to come up to the stage and have a try if you want to." So, this guy's friends were telling him to "go ahead up, try, try." This guy goes up, and Master Wong say "OK, you try and kick me and I will show you a technique and that is what happened.

The guy tried one kick, two kicks and then a side kick. Master Wong just avoid, and never touched him. Then the guy did a side kick and then all of sudden he did a spinning kick right afterwards. Master Wong rushed in and his fist was posed right in front of his face. Now at that time, Master Wong was around 54. The entire time only last about 10 seconds. I went to Master Wong and I asked him, "Master Wong, were you sure at the time?" Master Wong said, "I wasn't so sure, I just try my best."

DJ: I see that you have a very large school for Hong Kong, how many students do you have?

CAY: Enrolled, I have about 120 students.

DJ: I see also that you play music during class?

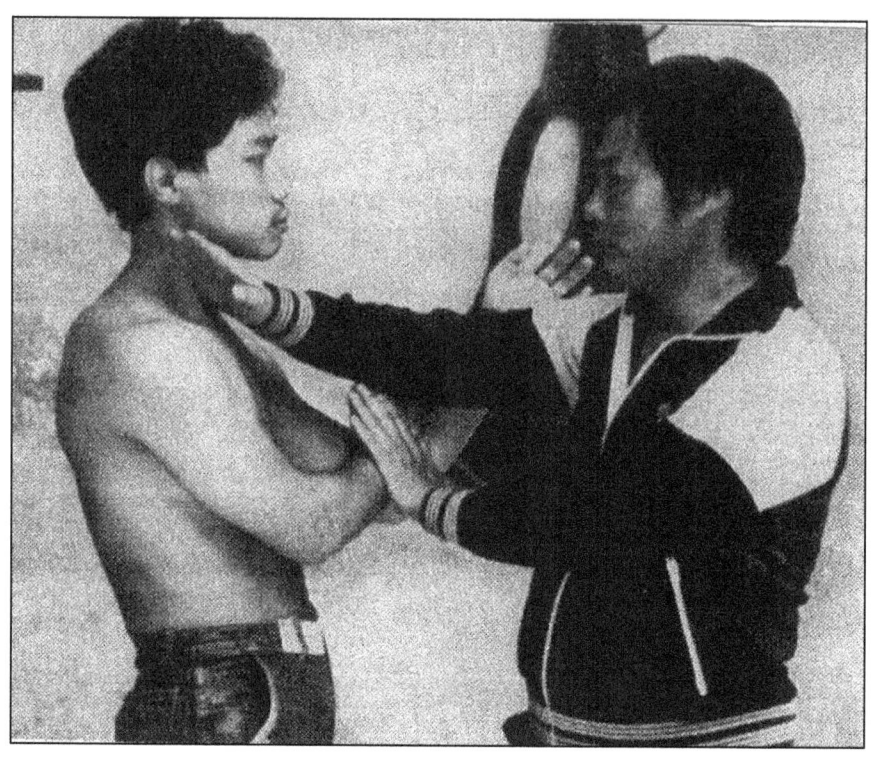

with GM Wong.

CAY: Yes, so a lot of places don't do that, so I do it. OK, to help attitude, to put them in a mood. To get them up and to help their concentration.

DJ: What is the first thing you teach your students?

CAY: I will work with them and show them warm up exercises. Then we will separate to different levels because each level has a different syllabus. The basic elementary level, I will teach them to punch first. Open the stance, and punching. And then later, I will teach them the 1st section, because in my opinion and experience, the Siu Nim Tao form is the most important. And the 1st section of the Siu Nim Tao form is quite great and important, so I let them know this and allow them more time in training.

Master Au Yeung with GM Wong practicing Lop Da.

DJ: So when exactly do they start to learn Siu Nim Tao?

CAY: Maybe 4 – 5 months.

DJ: That seems to be a fairly long time before they are taught Siu Nim Tao, what do they learn after stance opening and punching?

CAY: In Ving Tsun the form is just like a book, but it is practiced without the book first. So, I teach them practical movements first. When they train practical movements for a few months, I then give the Siu Nim Tao book to them.

And when they are learning Siu Nim Tao, I say, this movement you do just like you were doing a few months before. So, I think it is easy for them to understand and more easy for me to explain to them. When one of them first achieve the Siu Nim Tao form, maybe some person ask me questions, or I might have to do many, many examples so they understand. So, I teach them practical movements first, such as punching, Pak Sao, Gong Sao, Bong Sao, Quan Sao.

GM Wong with Master Au Yeung in Italy.

When it is OK, then I teach them Siu Nim Tao. Then I tell them this movement is from the practical movement from before. So, then there are not so many questions.

DJ: When you first learned from GM Wong, was that how you learned?

CAY: No, the traditional way. Siu Nim Tao for a few months, and then single sticking hand, at the same time learn how to step forward and then backward, and then later rolling hand. Like that.

DJ: How do you teach Chi Sao, in other words, how do you break it down?

CAY: It is according to their experience. Don Chi Sao, and then double sticking hands and cooperation with footwork, forward and backward, and then Lop Sao, Pak Sao, and then Luk Sao Chek Chung. I will separate them, I do not include it in double stick hand, only after 10 months to a year. Then I teach them to Chi Sao on small posts raised off the floor. It makes them balance and how to deal with a force. It is very important for a small guy or a weak guy. It teaches them how to put force to the side.

DJ: Now what exactly do you mean by "Posts raised of the floor?"

CAY: They are wooden cylinders; here I will show you. [Master Au Yeung went to the gym floor and brought out a round post about 8" round and 8" long].

Au Yeung with GM Wong Italy.

DJ: So, you stand on these and play Chi Sao, is this something GM Wong showed you?

71

CAY: Yes, exactly, I learned from Master Wong, he had this kind of training. I feel it was very good training for me, so I decided to keep this kind of training for my students.

DJ: When do your students learn Chum Kiu?

CAY: I will teach Chum Kiu from the 1st section, and before I show them the second and third section, I will show them some dummy work. For example, Bong Sao with a mirror, then partner, and then on the dummy. So, I take movements from the dummy form. I think this kind of movement to do on the dummy is to make you more accurate, and to correct it. So why not, why not?

DJ: How long will your students have to perform Siu Nim Tao before they learn the Chum Kiu form?

CAY: From Siu Nim Tao to Chum Kiu, around 4 – 5 months. Because from my understanding of the Siu Nim Tao form, the acceptance of the sections, it must be committed to memory. There are many movements to learn before and during.

Lunch with Cliff Au Yeung
L-R Brian Macdonald, Buick Yip, Author, Cliff Au Yeung

DJ: Is there anything else?

CAY: Yes Quan Sao, I ask the student to do it in front of a mirror and then a partner, and then to the dummy to correct. For me its different, because the dummy form is not a secret. It has a main purpose, to make corrections.

Of course, you always have a good partner, a good teacher to guide you. If you have no dummy, you can still do very well in Ving Tsun, sure. But if you can't find a good partner, but you want to keep your hand and feet timing good, and position, the dummy can help you.

DJ: And how long does it take from Chum Kiu to Biu Je?

CAY: More than one Year, my belief is the concept of Chum Kiu is quite different from Biu Je. The Chum Kiu form is for dealing with a street fight, one to one. Biu Je deals with a group of people.

DJ: Are you saying then that Biu Je is meant for dealing with a group of people?

CAY: You can interpret it like this. Biu Je say that you have no chance to win, but how can you survive? For example, more than one person fights with you, OK, you have less hands to meet them, or you get hit, or some people skill can keep fighting with you, or some people have a weapon against your bare hands, what can you do? So, it is for unfair condition. Where as Chum Kiu is for one to one, this is for fair condition.

Or one to one but your enemy has outstanding advantage, too tall, big, long arms, oh, what can I do? I can't run away. So I fight with you, maybe I have to use the Biu Je. So, Master Wong once told me that to hold your own in all the competitions, Chum Kiu movements is OK. One day if you use the Biu Je, it is for defeating unfair advantage by the enemy. So a student learns the Chum Kiu form, then if too quickly the Biu Je form is taught, then they mix up the two concepts. And in a fight maybe they will make a mistake.

Big mistake is that they can't choose the condition to use. So, you learn the Chum Kiu form, you are first stable training. Your movements are very good one to one. Then I teach you the Biu Je form. The Biu Je form the movement is very arguable in the Chum Kiu form. For example, in the Chum Kiu form, you never grab the hand, in the Biu Je form, always grab the hand. Oh, in the Chum Kiu form, we didn't use the elbow, in the Biu Je form, always render the elbow and use it. And the footwork is different. So, it is totally different, the concept is different.

DJ: I noticed that one of your students was practicing Biu Gwan with the palm of his leading hand facing up, instead of the more common way where the palm is facing down. Can you explain the difference?

CAY: To my understanding, the pole form is just like holding a gun, it is more stable and easier to move to handle it.

DJ: Did GM Wong show you this way?

Author and Sihing Buick Yip at Master Au Yeung's school.

CAY: Yes, Sifu show me. I learn the form from him. I know that some people do it with the leading palm facing down. Another thing that is logical, when the palm is facing down if you train a long time, it is easy to loose your grip because you get tired.

DJ Do you utilize a ranking system?

CAY: A ranking system, yes, sure. Red, yellow, green, brown, and silver, silver is for instructor.

DJ: It is interesting that you have a ranking system, because I haven't seen it anywhere else in Hong Kong.

CAY: I think it is a need in modern times because most youngsters and adults want to touch something. If you train 10 years, 20 years, when is finished? But with rank, there is separation, a few months, a few years, you can set goals, it is touchable, you see it. You can train under one Sifu and go 20 years and still be doing the same thing, OK, you come back tomorrow, you see?

DJ: Do you have advanced and beginning students train together?

CAY: Yeah, sure, the seniors help the youngest with new movements. But the senior even improves too, although the senior may hate it because it is too boring. But they learn at the same time too.

DJ: Where do you see Ving Tsun in the future?

CAY: I hope the people of the Ving Tsun world can get all the movements no matter so called traditional one, classical one, or the modern one. Put in front in a scientific way to make very objective, by geometry, by mechanics and physics. Because I know this way, we can get the real good Ving Tsun. I always say that Ving Tsun pugilism have a future because we can analyze the scientific way, and let them taste the truth to fight. So, if you are going to fight, to get the truth in fighting, use the tools, Ving Tsun is a tool, so it's a test to see if it works or not.

DJ: So, I think what you are saying is that Ving Tsun is not Ving Tsun if you can't apply it?

CAY: Yep. So, if it is to exist, no matter if so called classical, traditional, your own style, or modern style, OK, it should be the same. It was analyzed scientifically, and put to the test.
    Work is work. In Hong Kong, it is very hard to develop this. Maybe in America or Europe, the development of Ving Tsun has changed in this century. Otherwise, we can go back to the old way and say, "Oh, I have some secret movements, but for money." Rubbish! Work is work, no matter if it is the old style or the new style, because you want to prove that it works by physical test in a scientific way. Work is work.

Thank you Master Au Yeung.

DONALD MAK

Master Donald Mak with his Sifu GM Chow Tze Chuen

DJ: Can you tell us how you got started in Ving Tsun and why you chose it over all the other Kung Fu systems offered in Hong Kong?

DM: I was interested in kung fu when I was a kid. However, in the late 60's and early 70's, kung fu people gave a bad impression to the public in that they were Mafia. So, even though I was interested in kung fu, I did not start learning any kung fu until I was 17. When I was 15, I saw a Wing Chun movie called "The Warriors Two". I was so impressed with the actions and techniques shown in the movie. It was that movie that made me determined to find a Wing Chun teacher. Lucky enough, one of my classmate's brother's classmate, called Leung Ping Sang was Chow Sifu's student.

So, I was brought to Chow Sifu's school by this indirect relationship in 1979. Even though Hong Kong is a Mecca for kung fu, I have not practiced any other kung fu other than Wing Chun. Why I chose Wing Chun, firstly, it is because of Wing Chun's characteristics of directness, economy of power, using opponents force against them, flexibility, and close-range combat which is more suitable for my size. I am only 5' 6" tall. Secondly, I have such good luck to study under my Sifu Chow Tze Chuen. Chow Sifu is such a respected master that I have ever met. Chow Sifu is such a devout practitioner and master. Ever since he started doing Wing Chun in the early 50's and became Sifu in the mid 60's, he has never stopped practicing and polishing his skill.

Despite the fact that he is 76 years old now, he still practices Wing Chun and does Chi Sao every day. He teaches Wing Chun not for money! He teaches Wing Chun solely for spreading Wing Chun and keep the family tree of Yip Man Wing Chun growing. He used to work for the bus company, and he made use of his after working time to teach Wing Chun. So, he only teaches Wing Chun privately and never makes any advertisement for the school. My relationship with my Sifu is not that "buy-sell" relationship. That's why I can keep that relationship with my Sifu for over 20 years. Even though there are so many kung fu instructors in Hong Kong, it is not always easy to find a good master in terms of his kung fu technique and integrity. Because of my Sifu, I stick to my choice.

Third, it is not easy to practice and master well any particular style of kung fu. Since I have chosen Wing Chun, I want to dig out and master the most profound essence of Wing Chun that my Sifu always demonstrates to us. So I have devoted and committed myself to Wing Chun.

DJ: What was it like training in your early years with Grandmaster Chow?

DM: My training with my Sifu in the early days was like this. I learnt Siu Nim first and it took about one month to learn all three sections. Then he taught me single sticking hand. After about 2 weeks of doing single hand Chi Sao, then I started double hand Chi Sao. At the first month of learning double hand Chi Sao, we just did rolling.

After one month of rolling hand, Sifu Chow would lead us to apply the sparring and defending techniques learnt from the Siu Nim Tao form. I did these for about 8 months, then learn the Chum Kiu. Learning the Chum Kiu form would take me about 3 months time. After 2 years, he taught me Biu Je and which would take about a half a year. After Biu Je, I learned the dummy form, it took me almost 2 years time to learn the full set of dummy form. In about the fifth year, I learnt the weaponry, the Baat Jom Doa and the long pole.

Totally, it took about 3-4 years to learn the full set of weaponry forms. Amidst this, I was also taught the drilling like Lop Sao [grabbing hand], triangular footwork, Jin Kuen and Chi Gerk. Sifu chow would lead us to apply the attacking and defending techniques learnt from the 3 boxing forms, dummy, kicking and Baat Jom Doa all the way during Chi Sao exercise. The way of our Chi Sao is doing rolling and sparring alternatively. So, I completed the whole system in 8 years time.

DJ: Are Grandmaster Chow's training methods any different today compared to when you first started?

Master Mak with his Sifu GM Chuen.

DM: Curriculum wise, there is not much difference. Emphasis wise and teaching time wise, there are some differences. For example, Chow Sifu teaches much quicker than my time. Students of him can start learning the dummy form after one-year training with him. He put more emphasis on training of long-range combat.

DJ: I understand that Grandmaster Yip Man passed down to your Sifu a specialized kicking set which is performed on the wooden dummy. Can you explain what it is?

DM: This kicking set is actually the collection of kicking techniques from the original dummy set plus 3 more kicking techniques. The whole set is just the practice of all the kicking techniques.

DJ: You are the owner and Chief Instructor of the Hong Kong Wing Chun Institute. Do you teach any differently than Grandmaster Chow?

DM: Different people have different interpretation and experience. It is natural that I may have some things different from my Sifu. Having said that, I pass down my Sifu's teaching intact to my students. Anything that is from my own style and/or interpretation, I put that on top of my Sifu's teaching and tell my students that it is my added stuff. So, in a strict sense, I don't teach differently than what I have learnt from him.

DJ: In your opinion, what are the most important attributes to be developed through Ving Tsun training?

DM: Relaxation, centerline concept, Static elbow, simultaneous defense and attack, footwork and stances.

Master Mak at his school in HK

DJ: In your book "Willow in the Wind, Wing Chun's Soft Approach," you talk about the shoulder path. Would you explain this theory?

DM: The shoulder path concept is a key idea and foremost mechanism within the Wing Chun system for yielding to a stronger force. The key idea calls for the Wing Chun practitioner to lead the opponents force to fall into emptiness by using the shoulder path. Its fundamental principle is to use body structure and footwork to divert an oncoming attack away from the vulnerable areas of the body and redirect it towards the relative safety of the shoulder path. This idea is first adopted within the Chum Kiu form during the pivoting motion from the Ching Sun Ma to Pien Sun Ma stance.

DJ: You mention in your book the phrase "Ying Siu Bo Fa," - Structure neutralizes, footwork dissolves. Could you explain this please?

DM: This is a Wing Chun maxim. It goes "Ying Siu Bo Fa, Ying Fu Sung Yung," meaning, Structure neutralizes, Footwork dissolves, the opponents can be handled with less energy spent. This maxim points out the importance of good body structure and footwork.

Good body structure calls for:

a) Static elbow positioning

b) The use of the slanting body structure

c) The single weighted leg distribution

d) Waist springing

Good body structure allows the Wing Chun practitioner to yield like a Willow in the following manner:

1) Remain in the same spot while absorbing the opponent's strength into the Wing Chun practitioner's body through the creation of a force path vector directly from the receiving point to the ground where the opponent's strength is re-channeled harmlessly.

2) Pivot the body while controlling the centerline and guiding the opponent's attacks to fall onto the neutralizing shoulder path defined by the two-dimensional equilateral triangle where the opponent's strong force becomes harmless.

However, the dynamics of an actual combat is such that sometimes the Wing Chun practitioner must take a step, more so if faced with an opponent that moves swiftly or is exerting much more power than the Wing Chun practitioner's static body is able to absorb. This is where the use of footwork in the second part of the maxim "Ying Siu Bo Fa comes into play.

In our Wing Chun, the use of footwork allows the Wing Chun practitioner to remove his body totally from the path of the force or by following the direction of the opponent's force vector. The use of footwork requires the Wing Chun practitioner to move to a more strategic position from which to counter attack while keeping the body weight distributed 100% on the rear leg coupled with the shoulder path alignment.

The use of footwork in Wing Chun has other purposes. Its introduction expands the range of movements available to the Wing Chun practitioner to not only neutralize but close the gap, chase, adhere, stick and follow the opponent's movements in all directions. At the same time, the opponent constantly finds his movements cut off, restricted or falls on empty space without having the opportunity to use his strength to strike back at the Wing Chun practitioner.

DJ: When I observe people Chi Sao, it is easy to detect the tension and reliance on strength during this training. Would you explain in your words the meaning of relaxation and how to relax in Chi Sao? Also, do you consider Ving Tsun Internal or external?

DM: Proper relaxation is not the same as letting the body go limp. In my words, I define relaxation as "not using unnecessary muscular exertion that does not contribute to the efficiency of the movement in achieving its objective."

Master Mak at the VTAA

To me, Wing Chun is no doubt a "Noi Gar Gung Fu" [Internal martial art style]. Actually, by achieving the requirement of Noi Gar Gung Fu which will be explained in detail, can already achieve relaxation in Chi Sao. The debate as to whether Wing Chun is internal or external is mainly due to different definitions on what is internal or external martial art system. To me, and internal martial art is defined by these four criteria:

a) "Yuk Yau But Yuk Keung" - this means that the Wing Chun practitioner should yield rather than resist against the opponent through the use of muscular strength. The key word for this criteria is "soft," or being able to absorb and neutralize a strong force.

b) "Yuk Shun But Yuk Yik" - this calls for the Wing Chun practitioner to move in harmony rather than against the opponents flow of force. The key word for this criteria is "harmony" or join the opponents movement and from there lead the opponents movement into emptiness. It implies economy of motion.

c) "Yuk Ding But Yuk Luen" - this requires the Wing Chun practitioner to move steadily rather than erratically in order to maintain the centerline at all times. The key word to this criteria is "steadiness," or maintain the centerline in the face of an onslaught is crucial in the strategy of Wing Chun. Also, moving steadily and calmly rather than erratically. This also implies the concept of economy of motion.

d) "Yuk Jui But Yuk San" - this is translated into application to ensure that the Wing Chun practitioner is using his body mass properly by converging rather than spreading out his body resources inefficiently. The key word of this criteria is "convergence." The use of the Yee Je Kim Yeung Ma and body squaring allows the practitioner to focus his entire body mass by convergence.

From the characteristics of Wing Chun, it perfectly matches with the criteria of an internal martial system. So, I regard Wing Chun as an internal martial system. I also heard other definitions of internal style. It is said that opened-armed techniques of a style is classified external while close-armed is internal. From this definition, Wing Chun is an internal system.

DJ: Pole training today is obviously not suitable for self defense as carrying around a pole is out of the question. What benefits are gained from pole practice if not self defense?

DM: To me, any old-style weaponry in Chinese martial arts like spear, pole, knives, long bench, are not a way to compare with today's firearms. The value of weapon training in Wing Chun is just a way to supplement our empty hand techniques in the way of stance, positioning, and power. Pole practice can mainly benefit the training of power of arm and waist.

DJ: Can you explain what attributes are developed by each of the three-forms?

DM: Siu Nim Tao trains a Wing Chun practitioner's concept of relaxation, centerline, body-squaring and static elbow. It also introduces the basic Wing Chun stance Yee Je Kim Yeung Ma, and Wing Chuns basic defending and attacking techniques.

Chum Kiu further trains one's concept of shoulder path, single weighted center and Yiu Ma Hop Yat [concurrent waist and stance]. It introduces 2 more Wing Chun stances, Pien Sun Ma, and Ching Sun Ma which evolved from Yee Je Kim Yeung Ma. Footwork like Biu Bo, Tor Bo and body pivoting techniques are introduced in this form.

I understand that Biu Je introduces more deadly attacking techniques like Gwai Jarn, Man Sao, high low Guan Sao, Biu Sao, double Lop Sao, and Chap Kuen. Long bridge power and the other footwork techniques, Huen Bo are trained your particular method of Chi Gerk training is initially taught without holding each other's arms for support and balance, is this true?

DJ: Would you explain the basic premise of Chi Gerk training?

DM: Yes, we begin Chi Gerk training without using hands for balance.

The premise of Chi Gerk are:

a) cultivate the balance of the supporting leg.

b) train the waist, Kua and knee to become supple and smooth

c) Train the sensitivity of both legs.

d) Achieve the stage of using the hands and legs interchangeably.

The basic premise of Chi Gerk training is to have good single leg balance trained from the Chum Kiu form.

DJ: When training in Chi Gao, does your particular method of Chi Sao utilize forward energy consistently?

DM: If my understanding of Chi Sao is correct or the same as yours, we also use forward energy in Chi Sao. This is because Wing Chun's energy is a sort of penetrating and forward energy. So we also train this kind of energy during Chi Sao.

DJ: What aspects of Ving Tsun training do you have your students work on the most?

DM: Forms and Chi Sao.

DJ: In your opinion, what do you feel is the best method of bridging the gap to your opponent?

DM: Do you mean entry technique?

DJ: Yes.

DM: I like to use Biu Bo with Man Sao, or Biu Bo with Fuk Sao.

DJ: As with the long pole, the Batt Jom Doa training is something you wouldn't necessarily use for self-defense. Can you tell us the emphasis of training with the swords and what benefits are obtained from this kind of training?

DM: Weaponry can no longer be practical for self-defense. It is mainly used to supplement one's empty hand techniques in the way of the stance, positioning, and power. I remember my Sifu told me that when he learned the knives from Grandmaster Yip Man, GM Yip already told him that it was not practical to learn the form for the knives fighting or against any weapons. The value of learning the knives form was to blend the knives techniques, footwork, body positioning into the empty hand techniques.

DJ: You indicated earlier that Sibok-gung Chow teaches much faster now than he did earlier in his teaching career, that students learn the wooden dummy after being with him for one year. What do they learn in that first year, do they learn Chum Kiu and Biu Je?

DM: Yes, they do learn the three core forms before they learn the dummy. However, some application techniques and drilling like Lop Sao-punch against Bong Sao may be missed.

DJ: Do you teach any particular method of training waist power?

DM: No, I do not have any particular method of developing waist power. However, we specially emphasize on training the waist power from practicing the Chum Kiu and dummy forms that can help the development of waist power.

DJ: At what point is a student ready for free sparring in your school? Also, what is the process for teaching this?

DM: Actually, our way of Chi Sao is quite close to free sparring. Free sparring is our next step after Chi Sao called Lut Sao. Our Chi

Sao is divided into two parts, the first part is Pun Sao (Rolling hands) and the second part is Guo Sao [Attacking and defending with the Wing Chun techniques with one another). Please note that the Guo Sao is not preset or situational drilling of techniques.

It is a sort of fighting using the techniques within the boundary of Wing Chun. Both Pun Sao and Guo Sao still have contact with the partner's hands. Up to the Guo Sao part, it is already a simulated fighting. Our way is that we shall hit the opponent with the finger if a palm strike is used. If punching is used, we shall not grip our fist tight when the punch is touching the opponent's body. Hit on the target is still needed otherwise the practitioners will not know if they can really apply the technique or not. Elbow strike and kicking can be used when the practitioners have reached a high level that they can demonstrate their good control power.

Chi Sao is to:

– Reinforce the concepts or principles of Wing Chun,

– Train the sensitivity and flexibility of the body,

– Train the techniques of Wing Chun including the hand, leg, footwork, stance, facing, attacking and defending techniques, in a free flow manner,

– Learn the 12 hand to hand situations.

After some time of training on Chi Sao, about 2 years, if the practitioners can demonstrate they can reach certain level of the objectives of Chi Sao mentioned above, practitioners can progress to the Lut Sao stage, i.e., free sparring. Lut Sao means without contact with the opponent's hand, just fight in whatever way you like.

According to my Sifu, Yip Man always encouraged Lut Sao training. Yip Man had said, "Lut Sao Kin Kung Fu," (Meaning: the real kung fu can be seen from free sparring). So, free sparring is the last stage of training after Chi Sao. In my school, Chi Sao is trained every lesson because it is important training for using the Wing Chun techniques and concepts in a simulated fighting situation.

While free sparring will not be trained very often. It will be trained once or twice every three months. Free sparring is also not for beginner's level. The main reason is because free sparring can allow you to do whatever you like. If the Wing Chun practitioner does free sparring in an early stage and very often, one will not to train the Wing Chun stuff. Then it will become a free fighting training. It becomes no point to learn Wing Chun. However, free sparring cannot be skipped because it is the real-life situation.

DJ: Recap the emphasis for Chi Sao, Pun Sao, and Guo Sao for us please.

DM: - The sensitivity of the hands,

- "Listening" to the partner's energy ["Listen" is the traditional Wing Chun terminology for feeling the opponent's energy]

- Understand the 12 hand to hand situations,

- The proper posture of the three Wing Chun basic hand techniques, Tan, Bong, Fook.

- The concepts of relaxation, centerline, static elbow, [elbow down and in] body squaring.

- The practicing of simultaneous attack and defend,

- The using of distraction while attacking,

- Stickiness and control,

- The practice of "Luk Sao Jik Chung,"

- The training of using structure to neutralize and footwork to dissolve.

DJ: I have training aids for my students to train in Chi Sao, for example Chi Sao on a tabletop, and Chi Sao on stools. Do you utilize these training aids as well?

DM: No, we do not utilize these training aids. However, I was taught to practice Chi Sao on Mui Fa Jong (Plum blossom posts). The pattern is arranged like this:

```
    O   O

      O

    O   O
```

Each pole is of eight inches high and six inches round.

DJ: If there was anything you could change about Ving Tsun, what would that be?

DM: I think the Wing Chun passed down by Yip Man is already a complete martial art system in which it already contains the necessary fighting elements i.e. striking, kicking, grappling, and throwing. Besides, it's concepts and principles are so great that I don't think that I am great enough to change it.

Thank you, Master Mak.

LEWIS LUK

Lewis Luk school
L-R: Buick Yip, Author, Cliff Au Yeung, Lewis Luk

DJ: In your opinion what do you feel is the most important of Ving Tsun training?

LL: I think that I would develop into 2 stages. First is the basic, and I always think the basic is very important. I think that a lot of Sifus say that Siu Nim Tao is very important, because really Siu Nim Tao represent the basic of Ving Tsun. If you are good at Siu Nim Tao, actually, many of the important concepts and the majority of the things are already there. Chum Kiu, Biu Je, the wooden dummy and other things are to help you to develop further. So the basic is very important. And very often I find out that many of the students including my self in the early day's, do not spend enough time on the basics.

Like today, one of the new training that I learned from Yip Ching, as I told you, I have trained with Yip Ching for 11 years as a private student, is single hand Chi Sao, which is something I learned a long time ago. Now I go back, and of course now the single hand Chi Sao that I am training is no fixed pattern, of course the original single sticking hand has a fixed pattern, now is no. It is able to help you to use just one hand to you control the whole situation so that when you put up two hands together, it will be much more improved.

It is up to a stage where you think you cant progress any further in double hand Chi Sao, you just think, OK, I just stay there, I find difficulty to progress any further. Then go back to single sticking hand can help, can really help. But very often you find that the students are just too rushed, they want to learn more and more new things, they don't spend enough time on many of the basic things, like Pak and Lop Sao, this kind of basic thing, so first is the basic.

And then the second stage I think is very important. The student should open up as I told you, open their mind. Be more creative in their thinking regarding many of the Ving Tsun applications. Of course, what the Sifu has taught them is very important, because that represents the many years of experience the Sifu has. But one day you have to grow up, one day you have to be a Sifu, you have to stand alone yourself. So you have got to have your own thinking, your own interpretation, and open up more possibility on the application of the techniques you learn in Ving Tsun, and more importantly, to go deeper enough to understand the principles behind all of these techniques. As I say, every small detail, every small single technique in Ving Tsun has its own meaning. Of course, Sifu can tell you, but that only represents the Sifu's experience, and as I say, what I expect for the

Ving Tsun practitioner should be one generation better than the other, by that we should be getting better and better. That is an accumulation of experience of learning of different generations of practitioners. So, the student should be encouraged to develop themselves in a more creative way. So I think these 2 aspects are very important. One is the basic, the student should really spend the time doing it over and over so that it becomes very solid. The other is be creative, be opened minded to develop yourself, based on this basic, you know, how to understand more, open up their thinking regarding Ving Tsun.

Muk Yan Jong at Lewis Luk school utilizing a spring system for conservation of space. Note free floating rubber mount on bottom.

DJ: In Chi Sao, one of the most difficult aspects is relaxation. What is a good way to learn how to relax in Ving Tsun?

LL: I think still going back to what I say, very often you find that if a student cannot relax when doing Siu Nim Tao, he cannot relax when he is doing Chi Sao. So actually, doing it over and over again sort of develop a kind of habit on yourself. So many of the student start off playing the Siu Nim Tao using too much force, and it becomes a habit. So when you are putting on a Chi Sao situation as you say because you are under pressure, because you are more intense, you tend to tighten up your muscle. So, I think that a way to help is to be good at the basic. Another thing, maybe, some people think it is too much advance but I think it can be done, is to do the blind fold Chi Sao. What I mean by blind fold Chi Sao is the more senior guy opens up his eyes, and the junior one puts on the blind fold. By doing that, it helps you relax, because once you can not see, you will try and use your sense rather than your force. And sometimes the other thing distract you, what you see, what you smell, try to make you not tight.

That is my experience, and that is also what Wong Shun Leung taught at the beginning, he taught blind fold Chi Sao at the very beginning stage. But not like the others, one is open up the eyes one is closed, this time though, it is the junior who is closing his eyes and the senior who open up his eyes because he knows how to control and knows not hit the students to let him flow.

DJ: What are your thoughts on mixing other martial arts with Ving Tsun?

LL: Now I think that when you say it's mixing things, I don't like it. Because I think when you teach Ving Tsun, it is Ving Tsun, and Ving Tsun is very simple. It is one of the most simplest martial arts that we can find among the other martial arts. But on the other hand, I think that I can keep an open mind that as a Ving Tsun student or practitioner, he can go out to learn different arts, but respect that martial art as stand alone.

For instance, you also teach Shuai Chiao, but you name it Shuai Chiao, and give credit or respect to who taught you, and do not call it Ving Tsun or a kind of funny name which consists of all these different things mixed together. Even Wong Shun Leung, he used the term of supermarket approach where you go inside, and you got everything there mixed together. And many of the older generation don't like it.

So, my view is that I keep a very open mind and in fact I myself learned two different kind martial arts. I learned Ving Tsun which is my major martial art which I learned for the last 20 years, and I learned JKD under Tat Wong because I'm very interested in understanding what Bruce Lee was thinking about and of course I started to get some clue in which Bruce Lee was doing and I discussed with the older Masters what actually Bruce Lee was doing in the old days, and that he actually had his own plan regarding his own development of Ving Tsun.

DJ: I think a lot of it had to do with the fact that he did not complete the Ving Tsun system and he had to do it out of necessity in order to progress further. Do you agree with this?

LL: That is part of the reason, and it is a fact that he did not complete his studies. But another reason is that Yip Man at one time told many of his students, and one of them I think was Bruce Lee because some people say that Oh, why Ving Tsun has only 3 forms compared to other martial arts they have 10, 20 forms, so why so little, are you holding back something that you don't teach us? Yip Man said "You think that 3 form is too little, I can tell you that in future generation there will be somebody in Ving Tsun can make this three form into one form." That is in future the direction of Ving Tsun will only go to more and more simple, and not adding things more and more. Three forms will never become ten forms, the direction will be three forms to one form. That if you ask many of them, they know, so what I believe at least in the early days, what he actually doing was going in that direction.

Despite that he didn't complete the system, you know that Bruce Lee always had self confidence on him self. He think that OK, in future generation there is going to be one guy, it must be me. So, if you compare his curriculum in Seattle, Oakland and LA

Chinatown, and all the way along, he was actually going in that direction.

DJ: So how do you enjoy JKD, how do they compare to one another.

LL: I think there are so many things similar, on the structure side, that means if you look outside, it's different, the stance is different, the footwork is different, but here are so many similarities, and there are so many connections, and only by looking very closely, you will find the connections. For example, in Chum Kiu we have a punch which is driving like a cork screw, that is the interpretation of Wong Shun Leung for this punch. Of course, there are different people that like to do it like an uppercut, and in JKD there is one that is just the opposite of this, and so I think that he just twist it to the opposite.

DJ: Do you see JKD evolving any further?

LL: No, no, my approach, I learned from Tat Wong, I don't know if you heard that there is a difference of opinion between Tat Wong and Danny Inosanto, where Danny Inosanto is adding in Kali, and other things. Whereas Ted Wong is more of the original, and he wants to stay with what Bruce Lee taught him, and in fact what Bruce Lee taught him is very simple.

DJ: Back then it was really based on more Ving Tsun.

LL: Yes. So, I am more into the original one, more interested in what Bruce Lee is actually doing and not predicting what direction he was going, because he already died and there is no point in predicting what today if he lived what would he do.
  Actually, it is more important what would you do, that is if we want to evolve, if we want to change, we just change, we should throw away the name JKD.

DJ: From what I understand, Bruce didn't even want to give it a name.

LL: Yes exactly, exactly.

DJ: Where so you see Ving Tsun going in the future?

LL: One thing I find very interesting, if you ask some of the Sifu who you are interviewing to show some of their technique or their interpretation, you will find that each one of them has a different thinking, a different interpretation, and many people don't understand why.

DJ: Well, that's the uniqueness of Ving Tsun.

LL: Yes, exactly, if you don't have your own style, if you don't have your own interpretation, you still have not learned Ving Tsun. You still don't understand Ving Tsun, because Ving Tsun just give you the basic structure, the basics, and actually based on these basics, add in your character, your physical strength, your own characteristics, and then when you throw it out, it may be different. But I think that this is a good and bad thing for Ving Tsun, good things in that each person can develop his own characteristic. But the bad thing is because it come up with so many different interpretations some of the Sifu think that OK, I must stick with my interpretation, and mine is the only correct one, and the others are all wrong. And they don't allow their own students to share or to learn other things. Actually when you look at some of Bruce Lee's essays he said that at the beginning when some people find partial truth about martial arts, the founder is very good, but the followers try to make it like a bible and follow it as a rule that cannot change, they are putting in a grave yard for their founder.

So, I think that is a danger, because more and more Ving Tsun Masters they just want to make it very tight, you must do it like this, if you step one step outside you are wrong. And they never even think OK, there is more room in Ving Tsun, because Ving Tsun is very unique although you may not appreciate many of our terms, the names are very simple. This is Tan Sao, Tan Sao is just a strict interpretation in Cantonese even you are not using martial art, this is Tan Sao. Because when you say Tan Sao, it doesn't tell you what application it is, it can open to so many different applications. It just tells you the basic movement, and all this basic movement relates to you, the human being. I remember one time someone interview Wong Shun Leung, they say, OK, Chinese martial art very often relates to an animal, like tiger form, crane, monkey forms, so what kind of animal is Ving Tsun is coming from? Wong Shun Leung is very simple, he said that Ving Tsun is designed for human beings, not we want to imitate animals.

You don't have to imitate a cat, a tiger, or some monkey, you are a human being, so why don't you have a form for the human being? And I think that is the challenge in the future for the Ving Tsun master whether they really understand that that is the direction that Yip Man want them to go. One funny thing, Wong Shun Leung use Tan Sao like this, and Luk Yiu use it like this, and many people use it like this, and both of them go to Yip Man and ask which one is right? Yip Man said "both, are correct, sometimes your hand is here, you have to use it like that, and if it is here, you use it like that, it's that simple, you do it both ways." Yip Man is a very opened minded person, because he is one of the few masters that had the privilege to study in an English school. He came to HK and study in St. Stevens college which in those days, many of the foreigners studied there so he was open to western thinking and education. Many of the masters did not have the chance to meet this kind of education. I am trying to look at Ving Tsun from Yip Man onward. OK, before Yip Man I would be interested to study as a matter of history only.

But I don't mind nowadays that so many different kinds of Ving Tsun are coming out and claiming that they are older than the Yip Man approach, or more complete than the Yip Man approach, I think those are just irrelevant for us. Because what I understand or what I believe is that Yip Man already made good progress in Ving Tsun, he simplified, our system is much more simplified. We should not go back to the old days. OK, for a matter of the study of history, sure, so we can know where it came from. But as a matter of technique, we should go forward, not backward. Because there are many different Ving Tsun, they have 10 forms, 12 forms, many many complicated things, I don't think we should go back.

I don't know whether if people have talked to you about Batt Jom Doa, and you know what is Ba Kua (Eight trigrams), our approach, we already took away the Ba Kua, all the funny things about the I Ching, I Ching is good, but sometimes people go too much and make it superstitious. In the old days, people practice Batt Jom Doa against the Ba Kua, the reason why because in the old days, there were no mirrors, and when you practice Batt Jom Doa, there are only 8 directions, I mean you can only chop in eight directions. There is no other directions to chop, and if you want to learn and practice correctly you use the Pa Kua because it basically tell you the direction. But some of the Sifu didn't teach the students about the purpose of using the Ba Kua, they make it superstitious.

Today, if you go back to China, that some master in China ask, OK, you learn Batt Jom Doa, have you learned Ba Kua? If you haven't learned Ba Kua you missed out on something.

DJ: You are referring to the martial art Ba Kua?

LL: Both kung fu system and the symbol is originated from the I-Ching, the Book of Changes. It is actually a mathematical book; it's used for calculations for the future. Because Ba Kua yes, it is based on the I-Ching but the theory is very basic and simple. Bott Jom Doa eight cutting chop, that means no matter how many combinations there are only eight directions to cut, you don't have nine or ten. So, one hand is eight directions and the other hand eight, times together you got 64 different combinations, it's that simple. In today's knowledge of mathematics, you don't need Ba

Kua, everybody knows eight times eight is 64, you have eight directions here and eight here, mixed together you have 64. And you have the mirror and a centerline to use to help you to guide in the right positions, so you don't need the Ba Kua. I think for historical purposes; it is good to understand this.

Ving Tsun luncheon with the Grandmasters. Lewis Luk far right.

DJ: For historical purposes, what about the Look Dim Boon Gwan?

LL: Look Dim Boon Gwan, if you go to China there are many complicated Look Dim Boon Gwan, but our approach, is already down to the most simple, because I have learned in the old days how Yip Man learned the Look Dim Boon Gwan, originally he did not like Look Dim Boon Gwan because he thought it was too simple, so he learned other forms. When he got beat up by one of his seniors then he tried to really pick it up. Originally, if you go to some part of China, they only have the three and a half point, Saam Dim Boon Gwan, because that is the basic which is the Biu Gwan, Til Kwan, and Ding Gwan, if you can master these three, you have already covered 80% of all the attack and all the movement, because in Luk Dim Boon Gwan your side is the centerline, so if you face your opponent like that, no matter where he come from, up, down and Biu Gwan, and of course the other three and a half, Huen Gwan, Fuk Gwan Lao Soy Gwan, OK, and where do you have the half point? It's very simple, because all the six points are based on the first three inch that is the most powerful part of the Look Dim Boon Gwan.

But the Look Dim Boon Kwan has one weakness, that is if your opponent gets inside and gets too close to your first hand, that is dangerous. So, you have to learn from day one that if people go inside you have to take them out, and try to generate power between this direction so this is the half way, the half way through, the half point. Luk Dim Boon Kwan does not belong to Ving Tsun, originally, we have Batt Chom Doa, and you know in Batt Chom Doa we always cut the people front hand and cut their neck, or some fatal part, especially the front hand. So, we are always training to attack the front hand to make them drop the weapon, so we will try to keep our hand back as far as possible so we developed a half point to counter this kind position. If your energy is good, you can generate power half way between, you don't need the first three inch in the front, because the first six point cover these areas.

L-R, Lee Wai Chi author and Lewis Luk

DJ: So, do you believe that Yip Man was the one who simplified the Look Dim Boon Gwan?

LL: I believe so, because I don't believe that Lin Gai is telling lies, he is a very decent man, but when you compare their Ving Tsun to our Ving Tsun it is very different.

DJ: Who are you speaking of?

LL: Lin Gai, he is an early student of Yip man in Foshan China, he trained a group of students there. I think that when he came to Hong Kong for various reasons, he simplified the system, and I think this is good. He took away all the superstitious terms, like Yum Yeurng, Ba Kua, all this kind of things. You never hear of this in our lineage, but you hear a lot of this in other Chinese martial art systems, in fact I think that Ving Tsun is no exception, because Ving Tsun is one kind of Chinese martial art. Why it doesn't have, I think it have, but only Yip Man make it simple because he had the privilege to receive western education.

DJ: Do you feel that prior to Yip Man coming to Hong Kong in 49 he was superstitious in some sense?

LL: Not really, it was more political because he still had seniors and many of the seniors were still in Foshan and if he come out and teach differently, you would have ten fingers pointing at you, what are you doing, this is not what your Sifu taught you. This is the pressure he had in Foshan. They say there were 16 students and he was the youngest, so he had 15 seniors, looking at what he was doing in Foshan, so he could not deviate too much. So when he came to Hong Kong, he was the Grandmaster, he can do whatever he like. I think that is exactly the point that he tried to reform. I don't like to use reform, or modify, but he simplified it, to make it more simple, more direct, more to the point.

DJ: The direction of Ving Tsun students today is determined by the Sifu. Do you concur with this?

L-R Lewis Luk, unknown, Buick Yip, Steve Goericke, Andrew Ma

LL: Do you know that when Bruce Lee told the story of the finger pointing to the moon, that that originally came from Ving Tsun?

DJ: I never heard that.

LL: In Biu Je, the name Biu Je many people think it means shooting fingers. Wong Shun Leung told me and I should go into and research the actual book that it mentions Biu Je, Biu Je means "Finger Pointing to the Moon." That is exactly what Ving Tsun wants to do, as a teacher, you are acting like a finger, you point a direction for your students, but it is for your students to go in that direction. But not always concentrating on the finger, if you just concentrating on the finger, then you are short sighted.

So, I think that is the real challenge that means how open minded will be the Sifu to allow the student to develop themselves. Actually, I think Ving Tsun is a whole process of self-development, and eventually, from Wong Shun Leung point of view at the end of the day, you don't need the Ving Tsun name anymore, you are yourself, you have found the way.

Thank you, Master Luk.

LEE MOY SHAN

Author with his Sifu, Lee Moy Shan

DJ: Sifu, would you tell us what your view of Ving Tsun is for you and what it means in your life?

LMS: I took Ving Tsun to my soul. Everything I do, everything I touch, everything I see from my family to my business, somehow, in some way I relate it to the things that I learn in Ving Tsun. Well, somebody may carry Ving Tsun in a different way. Somebody may view Ving Tsun as the greatest fighting art. I view Ving Tsun as the whole world, of my inner world. I view Ving Tsun as a very good therapy for your physical health. I view Ving Tsun as a very good business strategy. I view Ving Tsun as a method to create a very happy family, and also the development of the human being in its own unique way.

So, since all of these theories and fighting structure that you teach, everything is very simple and direct. God, that's what this world needs! Just be simple and direct and that will cut off all the B.S. that surrounds you. If I want a business venture with someone and they are holding something back, then I am holding something back. We are not direct with each other, but if we are direct, business plans can exist in a successful way. If you open up a little bit, I open up a little bit. This wastes a lot of time, I'd rather say this is what I have, let's put it on the table, what do you have, heart to heart.

There is no successful fighting without physical contact. So, in your life look at your family. The only way to get a good response is with real physical contact. Hugging, caring, heart to heart sincerity, creating the best relationship, what a best friend should be. If one day you said, "I'm the man of the house, I'm the guy who wears the pants," Good bye to your marriage. That's the way the world is, learn from it, live with it, compromise with it. If you don't learn to compromise with these kinds of things, then you will have problems. So I view Ving Tsun as life. I don't know what other people view it as. If I want to get into a fight, oh, I'm sure I know how. Simple fact is, I have confidence. But if I want to create a good relationship, guess what, I know how, because there is a guide line.

My Ving Tsun, thanks to my Sifu Moy Yat, I appreciate what Yip Man Sigung has taught him and that I in turn receive this art myself. But I don't take this art for granted. I utilize it every second, every chance I get. There is only one guideline in my head, and that's Siu Nim Tao. Be simple, be direct, that's my concept of Ving Tsun, it's that simple. How other people view it, hey, they have their own development, because Ving Tsun allows you to do anything you want to do. As I mention to you guys many years ago, if you want to be an instructor, be one. If you want to be a fighter, be one, there are many ways to choose what you want to be. There are unlimited resources you can use, not based just on Ving Tsun alone.

**Out on the town in HK with my Sifu and Sihings.
L-R: Author, Lee Moy Shan, Steve Goericke, Buick Yip.**

I'm just saying you use the Ving Tsun theory, branch out to many different fields. Now, believe it or not, people who don't know Ving Tsun, they do it the same way.

Do you know how complicated this light is? [point's to the ceiling lights] They simplify it. All you have to do is flip the switch and the light turns on. Meanwhile in the back ground, you have to generate the power, wiring work, all this and that. All you do is flip the switch. Do you know how many years it took to develop that? Well sure, simple, but you have to have a plan to create that simple thing. So therefore, your life now beginning to train, plan, simplify things. Simplify your life. Really simplify your life. Life is complicated. All of a sudden you will find out that you can get along with people that you couldn't get along with before, whatever the reason is, it's so complicated.

But if you see people without color restriction, without ego restriction, without power restriction, without greed, you know now that you are dealing with a very simple factor. Just be friends. I don't care if it's black people, I don't care if it's white people, yellow or green. Who cares, I mean does that really make that much difference, because of my own ego?

Luncheon with the Grandmasters.
L-R: Steve Goericke, Chu Shong Tin, Lee Moy Shan, Chow Tze Chuen

Now we might be trained wrong in the beginning when we were a child, somewhere along the line we are told not to play with this color person because this color person is no good. Well, OK, when you are a kid you listen to your parents, and we face now our enemy. Isn't that stupid?

Now you're grown up, you're grown up to be an adult now, you will be able to justify what is right and wrong. Now you meet a different color person, now all of a sudden you say, they're not exactly what my parents said, or somebody else say's. They are different people, yes, but you know what, they have two hands, two feet, two eyes, two ears, one nose, and one mouth. They might not think the same way, but if we can exchange ideas, and really come across the bridge, how to learn each other's culture, what difference does it make? That's what Ving Tsun is all about.

DJ: Chum Kiu - bridging the gap.

LMS: Chum Kiu, what is Chum Kiu? A lot of people say, "Search for the bridge." What we wanted to say is "get across," learn from each other, in a peaceful way. What we are saying is close contact. Now Biu Je is "thrust fingers," everybody thinks it is the most powerful form in Ving Tsun. I view it like a compass. It gives me the direction of where to go. Now I get close to you, give me the direction of where to go. Two ways, either I can beat you down, or we can be the best of friends. If fighting, yes, give me the direction of how to best beat you down. In more peaceful time, give me the direction of how we can get more closer, and be best friends. Exactly like a knife. My Siu Nim Tao, I decide to cut an apple and serve you. Siu Nim Tao, again back to the beginning. So, these three forms, can they be separated from each other? They can't.

DJ: It's like Tan, Bong, Fuk, they are interrelated.

Annual Ving Tsun Weekend in upstate N.Y. Ca. 1980.

LMS: That's right. Now here comes the wooden man. That they take all the form and sectionalize it, and show you from the beginning, this part train what, this part train your hands what, this part train your hand again in different scenario, until you learn all 10 sections. Then you will say to yourself, let me mix it, put a, b, c, d, now into words, and then sentences. Then I say to myself that this is still no good, I need to write a letter so that people can understand. Then you do it empty, whatever you feel like. Now you learn from a to z, so therefore it is time for you to write a composition. In a peaceful world, you will utilize this empty hand Muk Yan Jong (Wooden man) for the purpose of writing sentences. In a fighting way, I don't even know how I will hit you, but because whatever you throw at me, my hands automatically know how to react, retreat, and take advantage of you if you make a mistake.

There are always two ways to view Ving Tsun, in the beginning, you only view Ving Tsun in one way, how to take your opponent down. As you get older, Ving Tsun really works into your bones, how to make peace. How to make your most violent fighting art into a very peaceful life. God, that's what it's all about! There're so many wonderful things in the Ving Tsun system.

You need your mind to discover them. I'm just here to guide you along, how to find them, which way to find them. You have complete freedom to do so. As you look at my Sifu's Siu Nim Tao, Chum Kiu, Biu Je, books, you see very little words in them. Why are there no words in there? Because you have to use your own intelligence to see things. You see it wrong, sorry, no teacher in the world can teach you, but if you see it right, you are one of a thousand, because now you use your brain.

These books were not meant to teach you, they were meant to give you some reference. This reference is all according to how intelligent you are, how deep of the knowledge you have of Ving Tsun to capture that.

How could you really teach people if they really don't understand it, or don't care? If they pick up the book, and since there is no words in there, they study really closely, that will give you a reference point. You do the right thing with it. By that time, you should have enough theory to be able to analyze it, to see why the routine is like this. I always advise people to challenge this, challenge this book. Think of the worst thing to defeat it. Don't forget that it has no words, so how are you going to defeat something that has nothing there? You see an object; you throw a punch and break this object. But if there is nothing, who are you going to fight? Yes, there is one person you are fighting, it's your mind. You learn how to analyze it now, so therefore you use your most intelligent way to defeat this.

If you could, your level of education is very high, if you can't, that's one of the books you put on the shelf and never ever touch again. That's why there are no words, there was a reason for no words. It's not just that we don't put no words in there. There is a reason for this, that reason is to give you the freedom to grow. Just a matter of you to learn how to capture them. Just a matter of how you utilize it.

A lot of people say hey, no words, how am I going to learn from it? They just missed the greatest glory there is. Hey! The air you can't see, how come you can live? Do you really need to see something to give you life? See what I mean? There's nothing there, can you see it, and you can't touch it. You try to grab it, but it leaks out of your fingers. You think you can get that much but actually you get nothing.

Think about that. If your enemy don't exist, do you really have an enemy? If you turn all of your enemies into friends, do you think you need to fight? No! That's the education of one person fight 10 thousand, not one person fighting one person. If you got 10 thousand friends, who do you think you are going to fight? But if you make one enemy, you have to face the challenge. It's gonna drain your body and will drain your mind. You don't create anything from it, there is no benefit for the people. But if you utilize the 10 thousand people to create things, you benefit the world.

Lee Moy Shan demonstrating chi sao techniques with Sihing Paul Field.

That's what Ving Tsun is really teaching us, how to be at peace. Well, sure you need to fight, there is a technique for you to use in a fight. But that's just on a low, low, low, level. When you get on a high level, you don't talk anymore. You'll see, you'll analyze, you'll create things that benefit us, people. You don't try to sell anymore. I never sell Ving Tsun, I work at it, and make sure it goes into my soul. I never say to people that Ving Tsun is the greatest, do this and do that. I don't say that, only that Ving Tsun is a way of life, if you understand it, you will receive benefits. If you don't understand it, maybe you try and learn something from it, but I am not going to push you to learn. I'm not going to push you, and I'm not going to say that it's the best in the world.

But there is one way you can create a peaceful and balanced life, if you allow Ving Tsun to work at your body. But if you shut the door, then nothing in the world can help you, because you shut the door yourself.

Now human beings are into more adventure, and so because of this, they want to find what's the best. They always think something is better. The best is right in front of you and they don't even see it, because it's too easy. Siu Nim Tao is too easy. From three year old to 80 year old you can do it, that's how easy it is. You take other exercise, either your too young to go through it or too old.

DJ: You mentioned last night that you should do the form for at least one hour, can you elaborate more on this?

LMS: My experience is if I drink this water and it's sweet, I will know that it's sweet. This is my experience after I do Siu Nim Tao for minimum of one hour. For half an hour, I feel nothing. I feel no rejuvenation. But if I do one hour, or two hours, I feel tremendous rejuvenation, number one, it sharpens up my senses. Number two, especially if I have a cold, my healing process is very fast. When I do Siu Nim Tao, I feel so much heat. After I finish, not only do I feel more awake, but when I go to sleep, I sleep like a baby. That will give me enough ammunition to face the world the next day.

These are very simple exercises I go through every day that everyone can accomplish. But a little higher, that will require a little more training. You have to discover that higher state, that's up to you. You are completely free as to how you are going to absorb it. Your mind now has so many techniques to solve different problems because your mind is clear. It is easier to solve problems because now you have the theories behind you. Be simple, and be direct, and then you will find a way to solve your problems in a simple and direct way because now you have a clear mind to do so. If you don't have a clear mind to do so, then how are you going to think? How is your strategy going to work? Nothing! So, what I experience, Ving Tsun, it is a working table for you to create many things on.

I don't view Ving Tsun as everything I view it as a tool, to create many different things. If I don't have a table to work on, how am I going to create all of the nice things? How am I going to write a beautiful letter? I have to have a table, Ving Tsun is this table. I hope I made this clear. If I were a heavy weight lifter, I could lift up 500 Lb., as long as my Siu Nim Tao tells me so. I could pick up 500 Lb., but I would have to go through hell to train this. I probably would have to go through several years of training to do this.

Because Siu Nim Tao requires you to satisfy yourself, to satisfy the body needs, to satisfy the challenge, so therefore he makes a point and he lifts up the weight to become a champion. That's the force behind these actions. Everyone has this force; it depends on how you want to use it. There is so much to find for you to become successful. That's why to me I view Ving Tsun as a table. It gives you time to develop yourself, gives you things to develop yourself. There are millions of Ving Tsun practitioners out there and everyone has their freedom to create whatever they want to create. So, some people can create without even a table, and that's even better. But I'm not that high level, so I need a table. That's how I view my Ving Tsun, and I love it, every minute of it. I'm not the most successful guy in the world, but you know what? I am satisfied.

DJ: You mentioned in the past that performing Siu Nim Tao affects your health positively. Could you talk a little on this?

LMS: All right, now we go into kung fu. We are the one who is supposed to build this structure. Build this basic foundation, utilize this knowledge to help create a better foundation, utilize this knowledge to create a better body, a better life. So therefore, when we train, we make sure the meridians are trained. When you start doing the form let's say for a half hour, you'll feel a warmth start to surround your body. And if you do it for one hour, you will feel this warmth goes even outside of your body, around your body, much more intensified. When that intensified heat surrounds your body, your body now begins to train, begins to create a stronger immune system, more powerful than if you don't do it. So, you have enough weapons to fight disease. Enough weapons to control the environment that continually attacks you. That's why we should not be afraid of dirt and germs, because these things make us work inside, to help the immunity system develop weapons against these things.

Without these germs coming in, our body is not going to know how to fight in the future. If nobody Chi Sao with you, how are you going to get better? So, this positive and negative always goes hand in hand. When you see bad things, that's what you learn from. They are there for a reason, that's why you learn from it, and train, create things that affect it. So human beings continue to evolve in this way. So, if everybody put their brains together, we could go to the red star. Hey, it's not easy to go to the red star, but if we all put our noodles together, nothing is impossible.

So, can you imagine taking care of your family, that's the easiest thing in the world. If you want to make money, that's so easy. You talk about ordinary life, that's so simple. In fact, you don't ever need to think about it. But what you need to do is train your heart and train your soul. If you train your heart and soul using Siu Nim Tao, you go through it a little easier. That's why I give my life to it, because I believe and it has proven to me that it works.

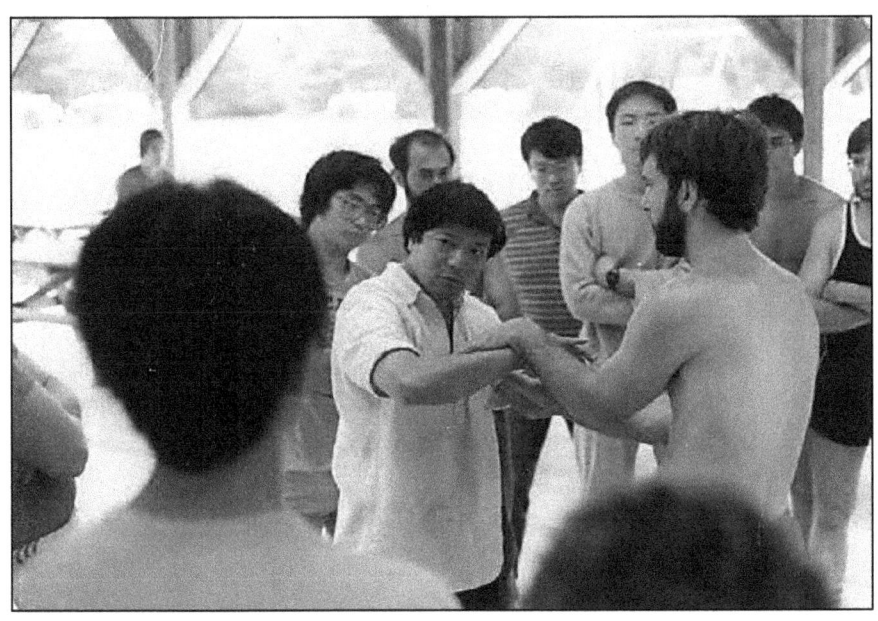

DJ: When one does a long Siu Nim Tao, an hour for instance, the legs have a tendency to shake or vibrate. Is there an explanation for this?

LMS: Earth element acts as a weight. If you pour a glass of water into a creek, the water will find its own path, and there is nothing you can control. When you stand in Yee Gee Kim Yeung Ma, you are constantly
fighting earth gravity, how your blood travels, how are your muscle, what is your balance and weight distribution, all of this is taken into consideration. Now after a while, you take a half an hour later, people who have not trained before, the legs begin to shake because they are running out of strength. The body is becoming very heavy, the earth gravity is constantly pulling at you, so you run out of strength, and when this happens you begin to shake and then you start sweating.

    Remember that water from the glass that was poured into the creek that goes its own way? Now your whole body goes its own way. Just let it go, let it be where ever it ends up. Because you

don't know where it's gonna go, you begin to discover things, because now you are beginning to look inside instead of outside. What do you learn from outside? Practically nothing but when you start looking inside, why are my legs shaking? Now you start concentrating on the legs, then you start thinking, quietly, now you start sweating, now you feel other things uncomfortable now. Look into it, you'll find things in it. If you don't use your Siu Nim Tao to look into it, if you don't even have a thought to look into it, then you will miss all the glory in there.

Those are very subtle things, hard to detect things. If you put your mind to it, if you make your mind into a microscope, you'll see so much. Now you are seeing yourself, the real you, who you are, how weak you are, which part is strong, which part is weak, what's your advantage, what's your disadvantage. When you start looking inside, it's better than watching a movie. But if you overlook it, what are you going to get? Hey, Siu Nim Tao is a very natural thing, just learn to utilize by looking in. Just don't concentrate, just let it be. Remember the glass of water, just let it be.

You drink it, it goes its own way, you can't control that. When it's time to go out, your body will tell you when it is time for it to leave. That's life, you drink that glass of water, it nourishes your life, let it be, don't control it. You breathe this air, let it be, don't control it. When you control it you hurt yourself.

I heard that a lot of people have many different ways to breathe. Well, breathe like when you were a child. When you were born you take that first breath and you don't know why. Of course, now you know why you breathe, to stay alive. Since now you know, do it better for God's sake, do it better, find a mountain and climb it, go back to nature, breathe in the treasure. You were complaining about people smoking right next to you the other night, you always complain about it. Learn how to accept it, fight with it, get it out. Then your kung fu will get better. Train your body to accept it and release it. Yes, people shouldn't smoke, but that is their freedom.

DJ: Some people complain that when they do a long Siu Nim Tao that their feet or legs go numb. Can you comment on this?

LMS: Feel numb, that means they had it, their body is telling them to stop, don't go any further, otherwise it may hurt you. Hey, you are doing the training, it requires time. It doesn't grow over night. I cannot put a person in there and expect them to do a one-hour Siu Nim Tao the first day, impossible. They ask for a little rest, sure, go ahead and take a little rest and then come back in. If I were to force them, they will hurt, there is no need for that. But if you train, really really train, I mean train for a purpose, train to fight, to be a fighter, well then you have to go all the way, just don't break yourself.

If you don't put yourself through hard training, your physical ability will not be able to accomplish the mission. Every little joint, every little part, every little toe, every little thing has to be trained, then you will accomplish what you want to accomplish. See how simple things are?

DJ: Sifu, does one reach a time in training with Ving Tsun where one becomes satisfied with their accomplishments?

LMS: Some people are never satisfied, I am satisfied. Satisfaction has no limit. Sometimes satisfaction can create a worse scenario. Well, maybe it's a good thing because you don't know when to stop. That's why human beings continue to progress. So it all depends on what you want. And my Siu Nim Tao, if I reach this level, I am satisfied, now if I had a little more strength to go, I might take up the next difficult challenge. To see who I really am inside, to see what my creativity can create. But then I no longer worry about myself you see, then I start creating for other people. My greed stops right there.

    I don't want power I want minimum satisfaction to satisfy my mind. And then when I am gone I am at peace. I have done what I could, I have done what I could to contribute to my family, to my marriage, to my friends, to the people that I work with all of my life. And I can contribute to many other people that I may not have ever seen. So, I said to myself, if that's the other fighting, hey, I'm doing it, I won't regret.

    So human beings as you can see, what the hell you learn how to fight for? Save your life, isn't it? But I want to save my life in a bigger way, that's all, not in a stupid fighting way. And this table can create many different ideas for me, and I grew what I wanted to grow. So grow what you want to grow, don't stop until you are satisfied, only you know when satisfaction has been achieved. I said this 30 years ago to my students, and I am still saying the same thing. And I am still doing the same thing, and the funny thing is that I don't have to do it that hard anymore now.

DJ: You made a big investment in the beginning.

LMS: Well if you want to call that a big investment, you know, there are many words to call that. If you call it investment, I don't complain. If you call it training, I won't complain, because you see, all work represents the same thing, right? See, I'm not a lawyer, so I am not picky with my words.

DJ: Sifu, would you talk about Chum Kiu?

LMS: What would you like to know in Chum Kiu?

DJ: Anything you would like to share with us.

LMS: You know the routine of Siu Nim Tao already, there is no shifting in it, it just trains your hands. Now Chum Kiu, if you really look at Chum Kiu, it's really just a matter of shifting. In a fighting way, you feel this shifting.

This shifting is not in a big way, this shifting is in a little way. Why? Let's say there is an object coming in, and you make contact, and you sense the object will go through you. Chum Kiu means the second you make contact; you just shift a little bit. But a lot of people misunderstand, maybe they step aside and then shift, hey, you that far off, you waste a lot of time. So therefore, that Chum Kiu come in just like this, that's enough.

If you analyze the whole form of Chum Kiu, different hand work, different foot work, they coordinate it, just to accomplish this little turn. To accomplish this little turn number one requires a lot of guts. Number two you are willing to take a blow because maybe you didn't train hard enough or good enough. Once you train good enough, no blow too hard for you in order for you to deflect it. Chum Kiu is really simple. Once you learn the Siu Nim Tao, now add in the little foot work, so you work basically the feet. Now you learn Siu Nim Tao, and now you learn Chu Kiu, and then your body begin to connect. Once they connect, you have mobility.

Once that mobility begins, you have a little more freedom. So, you look into Siu Nim Tao, you really don't have that much freedom because you are just learning the handwork. Now you add in the footwork, so therefore your upper body and the lower body make that connection now. In a balanced way, not in an ordinary twisting way. Balance, you have to discover what balance is. I show you the form, but go experiment, which way is the most balance for you. Some people believe that forward is balance, some people believe that leaning back is balance, and some people believe that in the middle is balance. Many different bodies, many different structure, many different mentality, so you find which one is the best one, the most correct one for you to balance yourself. Just like a surf board, you ride the wave you must be balanced. Everyone is different, everyone finds their own balance, of course there is a correct way to do it, that's where the technique is. Find the correct way, to find that truth is completely up to you. Because sometimes if I tell you the truth, your body is not accepting it. So therefore, by utilizing experiment, you yourself now discover what the truth of balance is. That's the fighting area.

Now in the life area, you learn how to balance the other half. How to balance everything around the world. People realize now that in ecology balance is very important. People in environmental work, balance is important. Now they start thinking of this balance in a bigger way because it involves a mass amount of people. So, you start small, go back to Siu Nim Tao, ask where do I need this balance, where do I place this balance, how do I balance myself so well that I don't trip or fall. That's Chum Kiu, very simple idea, see?

DJ: And then Biu Je as well has shifting.

LMS: Now you take the first form and the second form, now you have to create a little bit more don't you? Now the third form is the directional control, where ever that human being is, you have to have that directional control.

This directional control could be Doi Ying Joi Ying (Face shadow, chase shadow). You start from Chum Kiu, now you go into Biu Je, it doesn't separate it. From Siu Nim Tao to Chum Kiu, it was never separated, only added more. Now from Siu Nim Tao to Chum Kiu, these two now added into Biu Je and this creates another scenario.

      This scenario now is like a compass, where to go, where to go. That will complete your first stage of training in Ving Tsun. Let's say you graduate from college now, right, now what direction are you going to find a job? That's the difficult part. Now back to college, what did you learn, well I learned chemistry, now you have a direction to where to find work. If you finish Chum Kiu but not Biu Je, it is like you finish high school right, well, I'm gonna be a lawyer. You are dreaming, you know that's not possible because you didn't go through professional training, so your life now off balance. What you are thinking and what you can do are two different things. That's how I view my Ving Tsun, my dear darling little Ving Tsun.

DJ: All of your Todai's feel the same way Sifu.

LMS: Thank God.

DJ: You gave them the ability to think freely with it and to move in the direction that they wanted the best way that they knew how.

LMS: I'm not a dictator, I don't tell you what to do for a reason. If I do that, you will lose the freedom to create, and then you will miss the whole point. In the beginning, I might say you must do it this way, you have to do it this way in the beginning, and I explain to you why you have to do this. So you can search for the truth to find things that I said that may be wrong which will benefit you. If I don't give you the benefit of the doubt, you will never know what the truth is.

DJ: Now when you're done with the three forms you move on to the Muk Yan Jong.

LMS: They are all connected.

DJ: They are connected. Does it teach you how to connect the three together? What else does it train you in?

Celebrating Grandmaster Moy Yat's Birthday ca. 1980

LMS: Many people think that the Jong trains power. Yes, this is true, it trains your power. But more important, it locks in your Siu Nim Tao, lock in your Chum Kiu, lock in your footwork in a restricted area, centerline. And after you work in the restricted area long enough, and if you find your hands in an emergency situation, your hands will not make mistakes. They have been training in a restricted area, it's all restricted, everything is here. That's what it means. Moy Yat Sifu wrote a beautiful book on the Jong, yeah, there are not many words in it, but the first page explains what the Muk Jong is.

I think this is the correct way to do it. Not because he is my Sifu now, this is a tool for you to analyze, create your creativity. That's how I think, because what my Sifu say I respected very much, and I use my brain, always try to analyze. Will that benefit me, will that be useful for me? And I find out that my thinking and his thinking very similar. Like everyone else, I always have a question mark, I always have a question mark in my brain. Why I have to do this, why I have to do that, there is a reason, isn't there? So that question is, What? Well, let's find out, take it down piece by piece. Let's analyze like an engineer. When you start to analyze like an engineer, then you will discover what benefits you, and what does not benefit you.

So that wooden man is to utilize what you have learned. Your hand work, your footwork, your directional control, now you use the wooden man until you are free, until you know it so well you know it backwards. Then the wooden man is complete in your soul, inside of you. You must do it without thinking, in the beginning of course you must think. It's just like a new student, you think, you think, until you think so much that you understand everything, and then you don't even think about it anymore.

Then we go to the next level, now let's do it without the wooden man. Now you write a conversation with your head, your mind, so you can do anything with your hands and feet. So, the second you make contact with your enemy, hand and feet react so well that it surprise the heck out of yourself. Because now all of this training has become automatic. You have no more Siu Nim Tao in your head, you have no more thinking in your head. So therefore, you can even close your eyes and fight. Now some people call it the highest level. I don't think so. That's just the beginning, you just finished college for heaven's sake. You have no experience.

You have enough tools to know what is right and wrong. You have enough tools to know how to protect yourself. Now you go out and get experience. That's what it's all about. That's why I always say fighting is one thing, experience of life, exactly the same thing. Now better yet, there are theories. Ying Da Jut Da, Butt Ying Da, Butt Noi Da, Mo Guerng Da, Mut Learng Da. (If I want to hit I will, - if it's time to hit, hit, - if it's not, I won't, - don't force yourself to hit, - don't be sloppy) These are the most important theories, those most important to guide you along when to do things and when not to do things. I think that is the most difficult thing to train.

And then "Da Sau Chek Siu Sau" your hitting hand is your defensive hand. These are the hardest things you can ever do.

Until now I am still learning. When to go and when not to go. You know, these are hard, I am telling you right now. And yet, they are not hard like it is impossible, and if you really think about it, if you just put that little sentence in your head, every time you want to do something, now it becomes easy.

If you just do it with your emotion, that is hard. You understand it, you utilize it, and you use it at the right moment, now it becomes easier. That is the beauty of Ving Tsun. Every time I talk about this my heart is warm, I cannot say thanks enough. That's why I am what I am. I mean there are a lot of famous Sifu out there, they must think either similar, or better than me because they train longer than I have. They utilize the life structure better than I am. So, if I can find these people, I still can learn something from them. I don't restrict it to myself because number one, I don't have an ego problem. I don't say, hey, I learned enough, I don't need to learn anymore. I don't have that problem. I don't have greed, I don't want fame, I want to be myself.

DJ: That's what Ving Tsun allows you to be.

LMS: That's what it allows me to be. That's why I am glad you guys are learning this, to create yourself, utilize my experience. I have good experiences and bad ones. Hey, learn from my bad experiences too, so you won't have to go through it, what I went through. You know that is why we are like a family. Family is important, that's why they talk to me, and I talk to them all of the time. Learn from your Sifu's mistakes, so you can be better than him. So every time you go to sleep, give five minutes of thinking about what you want to be, and work it out step by step.

DJ: That's what Ving Tsun allows you to be.

LMS: That's what it allows me to be. That's why I am glad you guys are learning this, to create yourself, utilize my experience. I have good experiences and bad ones. Hey, learn from my bad experiences too, so you won't have to go through it, what I went through. You know that is why we are like a family. Family is important, that's why they talk to me, and I talk to them all of the time. Learn from your Sifu's mistakes, so you can be better than him. So, every time you go to sleep, give five minutes of thinking about what you want to be, and work it out step by step.

DJ: Sifu, what is your advice for people just starting out in Ving Tsun.

LMS: Patience. You don't have that patience; you will get nothing. I see a lot of failure because of no patience. They want to be the best overnight. If that's possible, be my guest, I can't do it. I'm not the kind that can be successful overnight. I'm the kind that requires hard training and patience to accomplish what I need to accomplish. You know, number one, patience, number two, not lazy. You set up the things to do, and then you go do it. If you think of the things to do but put no action behind it, what are you going to get? Nothing.

So, whatever you think of, you have to put action behind it, otherwise you're just dreaming. If I have anything to say important, I think this is the most important thing I can say. You think of throwing him a punch, if you keep on thinking [He laughs] he's gonna come back and throw you a punch. Action! All things are successful because of action. Of course, planning. Patience is to give you the time to think, and plan things out, then action follows, then you accomplish what you want to accomplish.

DJ: Is there a preferred breathing pattern when practicing Siu Nim Tao?

LMS: Just breathe deeply, and let it all the way out to let the carbon dioxide that is harmful to you fully escape your body. The best place to do it is in a very fresh air environment. So, when you breathe very deeply, now your lungs expand to the maximum, and then when the lungs retreat, all the carbon dioxide will expel from the body. So, you repeat this over and over again. Like this, you pick up 500 Lb., the first thing human beings do is breathe deep, very deeply. And then after a few rituals like this, then they begin to pick it up. What does that tell you? Every cell, everything is renewed before you attempt to pick that up with your full strength. You just can't get up in the morning and pick up 500 lb., be my guest if you can do it. But I guarantee something will be hurt. If you are hurt it is caused by your ignorance, your education.

I tell you guys many many years ago to go back to Siu Nim Tao. Go back to your Siu Nim Tao. Moy Yat Sifu always tell me Chu Shong Tin is the best Siu Nim Tao player. I do believe it because this is so important.

DJ: Are there any particular methods of training to enhance your abilities in Ving Tsun?

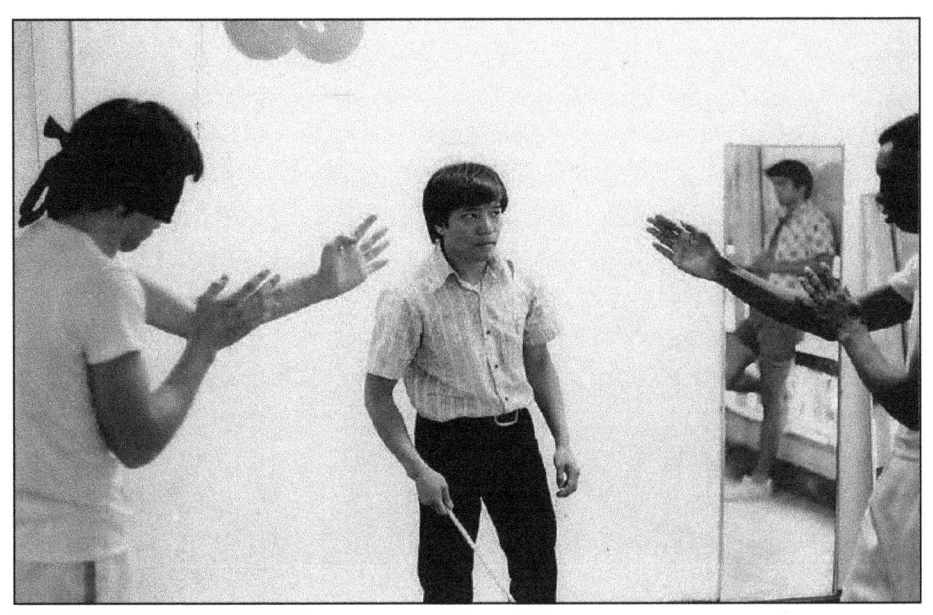

Lee Moy Shan instructing in Blind Fold combat circa 1974.

LMS: You want to take it up to the sky? More work. You want to dedicate one-third of your life, which is 8 hours a day constantly doing Ving Tsun, then it will carry you to the sky. Time, jammed packed time, not spread out.

DJ: I remember when I was training, we had to light an incense and do Siu Nim Tao to the incense before we could do anything else in class.

LMS: I don't make you guys do that to waste time. I do that to see what development stage that your body needs. So, when they do that, I go to the office, every once in a while, I peek out to see which one had enough and sit down, let's see which one needs a little bit more training. And then in my mind I will have a routine for this particular person to do. So, as you know, I train everybody differently, well not differently, but individually, same exercises, loosen up, warm up. But Chi Sao now, that is different. Tall one's, short ones, there will be problems unique to each person. So I must guide them in the head what to do, and then I walk away and let them figure it out.

This is important in that area, you are dealing with so many different people, different heights, different mind sets, different levels of understanding. Even Siu Nim Tao, it's funny, I teach Siu Nim Tao one way, and I find 10 way coming out differently [we laughed]. And then you go over to another school right, and you say, hey, my Sifu didn't teach it that way, where the hell did yours come from? We try not to see those things, there's no such thing as right or wrong in those areas. I teach it one way, you learn a little different, it's my fault? It's just your level of understanding is not like mine, and I don't knock it. Is it really that important? No, it's not really that important. Somebody decide to do Siu Nim Tao like this, and some may do it like this, [Shows variation of Huen Sao] as long as he understands that he teaches it the correct way, that's fine. But don't teach people the wrong way. Now the funny thing is the student learn the wrong way, and someone comes along, he feels comfortable and all of sudden he is corrected. Can you figure that out?

DJ: Well they usually get that figured out in Chi Sao. Speaking of which, in your opinion, what benefits are derived from practicing Chi Sao? Now I remember what you used to tell us all of the time, and I repeat it to my students. Since I have a student here now, maybe it would be a benefit if he heard you talk about it.

LMS: Chi Sao is a wonderful thing. I'll tell you how wonderful it is. You know there are so many different kinds of people, somebody mean, somebody strong, somebody weak. In Chi Sao, you feel everyone's temptation, your feel everybody's temper, you feel everyone's weakness, and you especially feel everyone's ego. You feel all of those things the minute you touch hands, oh, this is this character, and then you touch another person hands, oh, this is that character.

It's like going to the movies, different scenes all of the time, not boring. So never play with the person you like the most, always taste everybody, in Chi Sao, anybody comes along, welcome, I need to learn you. I need to learn who you are, and what you are thinking without speaking.

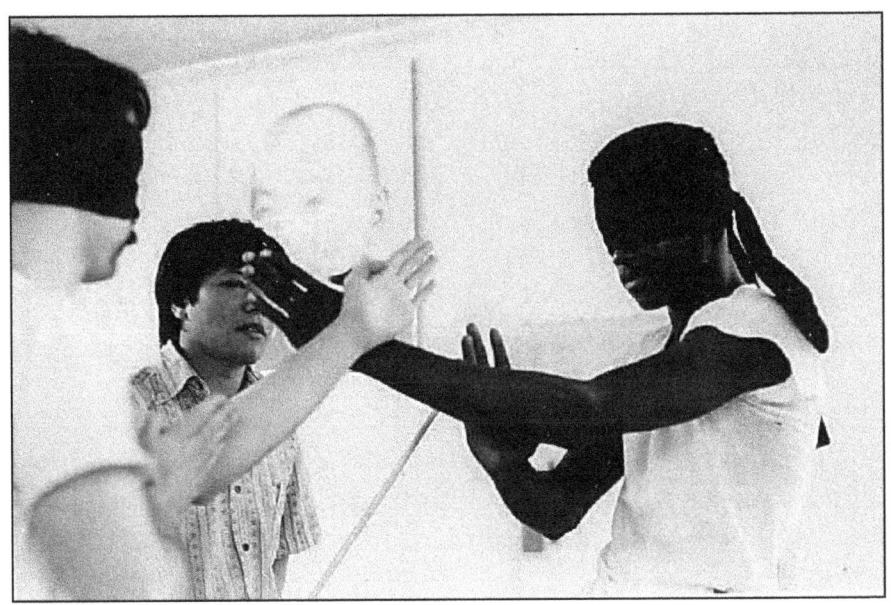

DJ: And you can't be afraid of it.

LMS: Absolutely, it gives you confidence, you never ever had this kind of confidence, you will never get anywhere. So now I meet Brian, I already know who Brian is without you knowing how I even know. That puts me a little step ahead of other human beings. You do Chi Sao with 10,000 people; your education of people is even greater. When I do business, the minute they walk through the door, I watch them like a hawk. I already know what he wants, and I already know what kind of technique he uses to convince me. Isn't that scary? It is wonderful you know in advance.

DJ: So that's what Chi Sao does for you. It trains in you the ability to interpret people. It evolves from a touching factor to no contact.

LMS: Hey, you touch so many mentalities, you touch so many souls. Hey, it's not like you see me, you've seen them all. You see a thousand, now you're talking.

BRIAN: So, you learn how to translate every little aspect of Ving Tsun into...

LMS: Life! That's why I said, Ving Tsun is like a table, it is a most important tool for you to experiment with. Without that you will have no chance. Now I am not saying that Ving Tsun is the only thing in the world, OK. There is a beautiful universe out there that can teach you a lot, how to make a living, OK.

But with all this education if you don't have a spiritual soul, what good is it? See, the beautiful thing is that Ving Tsun is not a religion, but yet it teaches you how to help people, it teaches you to be in touch with people, and it teaches you how to be at peace with people. It will also teach you how to not take advantage of people if you allow it.

Of course, if you have a teacher that teach you violence, beat them up, kill them, you will end up a violent person, you see? Ving Tsun doesn't do that. Ving Tsun always reflects on two things, situation, & life. You see, I put Ving Tsun in life first, some other Sifu may not want to do that. That's why you have the opportunity to grow the way you want to grow. My opportunity to grow is how to make peace with people through this violent art. See, that is my interpretation of it, that's not what Ving Tsun is. Ving Tsun is the ability to create what you want to create. I choose this way because I believe and have done my experiences through this way. Just your mission to accomplish it or not is all up to your Siu Nim Tao.

DJ: It seems to always go back to that.

LMS: Isn't that sickening? [He laughs]

DJ: Well no, it's not, because when you get lost you can always go back for reference. Everybody just wants the newest thing and then they don't practice Siu Nim Tao anymore.

BRIAN: That's because they don't see the depth to it.

LMS: You just said the right word. That is the best word for it. This Ving Tsun has depth to it. That's the level that creates our human being, create our life. The very, very depth of our psychological thinking. Not anything, I say, hey, if it was not interesting, why listen? Because what I say has depth inside, can wake up your soul, could wake up your spirit, wake up our joy, wake up your beliefs. Then you listen, don't you?

    I didn't create it, some people a few hundred years ago create it and pass it on to me, that's why I am thankful to them. I have no capability of that kind of intelligence. But once I learned it, then I utilize it. When I utilize it, hey, wow, thank you. That's all I have to say, and that's all I could say.

DJ: You would have us do a lot of single leg for balance training, putting shot glasses of water on our knee, or a quarter...

LMS: Single leg is great at developing your balance. Now you are no longer on two feet, but a single foot. Now all of these muscles in the ankle and leg are twisting, flexing and turning until you stabilize. Then you have a greater balance, a more stable balance which give you more achievable maneuverability now because you have the strength to carry the entire body on one leg. That's why train individual leg.

DJ: Why is it that we squeeze the fist tight while it is in the chamber when performing forms work?

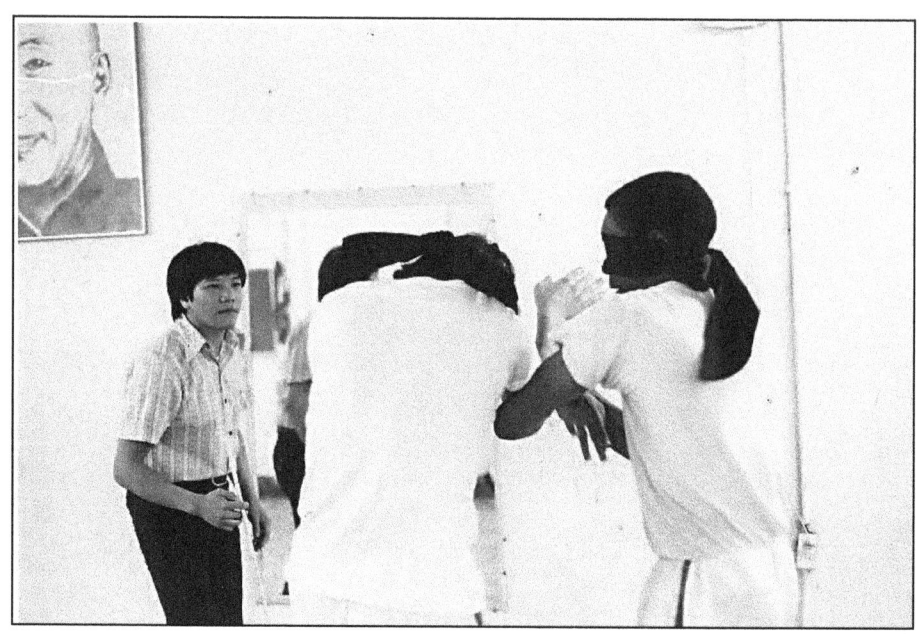

LMS: Ving Tsun on one side remains in the chamber when doing the form, and it's harder than the other side. According to Moy Yat Sifu, this is for training, discipline your correct position. So, this side is thrust out and is full of energy. The other side is hard and if you release it from white to red [When squeezing the fist as hard as you can, the blood is pushed out and your fist will turn white] there is motion going through. There are blood streams, there is a force of penetration because you block this force and then you let it go.

When you block this force, everything is backed up inside like a traffic jam, and when this traffic jam is finished, you see the cars are going all of a sudden 60 miles an hour. So the fist in the chamber held tight is like this traffic jam. Training, training to hold your punch hard when you make contact.

DJ: So this would be considered Yin and Yang, one side relaxed and the other side hard?

LMS: Some people translate it like that. We don't translate it like that. We will simply translate it in this way, this [Hand chambered] is training ready for explosion, and this going out for protection. Training, not the actual situation. You cannot hold the punch hard all of the time or you waste the energy. So you hold it loose, but when it comes time for contact, all this training, it's already built in.

DJ: Sifu, I know I kept you here for a long time, but I have one more question before we go to dinner with everyone.

LMS: Be my guest.

"Look at this guy, he's taking another picture!"

Out on the town with
Lee Moy Shan. L-R Brian MacDonald, Buick Yip, Steve Goericke

DJ: Is there anything you miss from the early days when you had your school?

LMS: Do I miss it? Life is changed every second on the second you know. Oh yeah, I miss you guys, but I have the ability to pick up the phone and call you guys, so why would I miss it? It's different, times change, you don't go back. The only thing that keeps on going is we build our relationship over the years together, and we didn't disappear. That's important.

    I hope this conversation helped you guys, because sincerely from my heart, it helped me, and sincerely from my heart, if it helped you, then use it. I'm not saying that I am all right, things that I can do you may not be able to do because of different situation.

Thank you, Sifu.

Douglas Lee Moy Shan *C.* 2016

DR. WONG MOY PING

**William Wong in foreground – Kenneth Scala in back.
Ding Leg School *Ca.* 1975**

DJ: Can you give us a short background on your personal history?

WW: Being that my dad was a sailor and stationed in New York City, I was born on the lower west side of Manhattan at the old St. Vincent's Hospital in the '50's and raised in Brooklyn during the racial conflict days of the '60's. At age seven my friend and I was set upon by a black gang of junior and senior high schoolers and beaten for our Halloween Trick or Treat candy. At age 11, going home to lunch from school another gang of blacks again mugged and beat me for my pocket change. At 12, I was held with a knife at my throat by a Puerto Rican for the few cents I had been given to buy a Sunday newspaper for a nun who was one of my teachers.

DJ: What, if any, prior martial arts experience you had prior to studying VT and if so what system and who was your instructor and how long you studied for?

WW: By August of that year, 1966, I started training in Karate at the studio owned by Professor Florendo M. Visitacion, aka *Professor Vee*. It was an absolute honor for me to have spent time speaking to and observing that great grand master. He knew so many martial arts starting with the Ju Jitsu he had taught to WW2 Marines at Parris Island, combined with karate, Japanese and Philippine blade and stick fighting. The man was humble in the extreme while awesome in ability and his demeanor created for me the image of what a martial arts grand master should be and behave like.
After moving to a different part of Brooklyn in '67, I again had the honor to study with another great teacher, Russell Kozuki a 7 Dan in Jujitsu and 8th Dan in Hawaiian Kempo he titled Goshindo Kempo. "Mr. K" had been a highly decorated member of the Neisse 442 Regimental Combat Team, the all Japanese Regiment in the US army, who fought in Italy and were one of the most highly decorated and combat experienced units of the Army.

DJ: How were you introduced to Ving Tsun as well as who your Sifu is, when did you start training including the location and are you a disciple of your Sifu?

WW: By 1973 or 4 a childhood friend and fellow Mr. Kozuki student John Cheng, (Cheng Moy 4), introduced me to Sifu Moy Yat. I became a "special student" i.e. disciple of his and became known as Wong Moy Ping #25. The school, Ding Leg (named after the urn Shaolin students had to move to get initiated up from student status to monk status), was located in an apartment on the ground floor at 5 Parkside Ave., just across the street from Brooklyn's Prospect Park. We had a very rich martial arts community in the general area with not only our school but another Wing Chun school run by Master Jason Lau a Wing Chun man from Jiu Wan's linage. There were also assorted karate schools in the area most notably Jerome Mackie's, on Flatbush Ave. near Church Ave. Mackie's school was among the oldest MA schools from the judo craze of the 1950's.

DJ: Who were your classmates at the time and what do you recall most about them?

WW: There were 24 disciples in the special student linage before me and they represented a cross section of cosmopolitan NY. Italian English teachers, Puerto Rican and Jewish ex heroin junkies now super clean, Chinese born Chinese (aka CBC's) with various forms of martial arts experience from Hong Kong. ABC's (American Born Chinese) with mostly a karate and ju jitsu background. Most notable to my recollection are Lincoln, Micky, Lester, John Cheng, Dale Green and my two closest brothers and invincible fighters Kenny Scala (then Kenny Canteriucho) and Eddie Soto.

DJ: Who was the person you worked out with the most and why?

WW: Gosh, we would round robin Chi Sao with all hands there and we were rough about it. In one intense Chi Sao session John Cheng left the sides of my neck, chest and forearms so purple / black and blue that my girlfriend freaked at my appearance! But if I think on it hard enough, I spent most of my time at Ding Leg with Dale, Kenny and Eddie. Our personalities meshed and we had many shared interests. Dale was the son of a chemist who'd invented a super expensive car polish / protectant that worked beautifully. Dale had followed his dad into chemistry and always carried a glass Binaca, (breath drops), bottle full of nitroglycerin he's cooked up in his bathtub. Kenny and Eddie were born street kids and street fighters and were the best actual fighters Din Leg ever turned out.

DJ: Do you recall any practitioners from other systems coming into class and issue a challenge?

WW: While at Ding Leg, none of the students issued a challenge but we did have an open feud with Master, Duncan Leung and his students. The dislike between my Sifu Moy and Leung went back to Yip Man's school where Sifu had been the school scribe, maintaining the school history and books, while Leung had taken William Chung's place as school fighter, the one who fought challenge matches against other schools. Moy didn't just dislike Duncan he despised Leung. The animosity between the schools would have led to blood shed as being extremely driven, the two schools were ready to take each other on with Yip Man's favorite weapon, shotguns! It was Master Duncan who somewhat diffused the situation just before we get in serious trouble by coming over to Ding Leg uninvited with two or three of his top students and we all had a good talk and took our energies out in Chi Sao. To go into another teacher's school uninvited is in itself a challenge but my Sifu swallowed hard, was gracious at Duncan saying he wanted a rapprochement. Both the teachers got to speak to us and then we had a Chi Sao match their best against our best. John Cheng and Eddie Soto were our absolute best. I think Micky fought then also. Eddie held his own and fought Duncan's top man to a draw. John did well overall but did get bounced off the walls three times, much to his and our shock. There was also something about the street wise way Duncan spoke of techniques and the scars visible on is forearms, (put there by an Eagle Claw fighter), that spoke to his real-life fighting experience. When he spoke, his suggestions were not academic and theory, they were demonstrative of his combat experiences. Some of the challenge matches in Hong Kong were fought to the death or serious injury.

DJ: What was your favorite training aspect in Ving Tsun, e.g. chi sao, form work, dummy etc. and explain why?

WW: My favorite aspect of the art has changed as I've progressed in it these last 40+ years. At first the Chi Sao and how being rough and good at that made street fights unbelievably easy and short affairs! As I've become older, I realized that the name Sil Lum Tao can be looked at two ways; the most familiar way was "Done with Little Thinking" or it can mean the "Sil Lum Way" Sil Lum being the Cantonese name for the Shaolin monetary. As I progressed through the years, I learned to draw in chi energy both from the ground and the ethers while doing Si Lum Tao and the other forms. Leading me to better understand the soft energy that's needed to apply the Bil Ji strikes. As I see the progression of energy in Ving Tsun from hard external energy to soft internal energy a graph of it would look like this:

Lester Lau on the right. Ding Leg School *Ca.* **1975**

DJ: Have you ever had to use your Ving Tsun outside of class, please relate the story?

WW: Yes. Had an incredibly long and heavy Hungry Fist period to my Ving Tsun. Street fights, bar room brawls, challenges, I've had more real fights with no rules, no safety gear, fighting to serious injury than I have fingers and toes to count them on. And, further I have to say that while I did karate, my win to loss ratio was about 50/50 but since fighting with Ving Tsun, I haven't been hit once, and have ended most of the fights with me landing just one blow. No brag just fact.

DJ: Can you describe to us your personal understanding of Chi Sao and what the emphasis should be while practicing it?

WW: Chi Sao should at first teach a student to protect his centerline and to parry away intrusions into the centerline while countering and continuing to press the attack. After the basics are learned, Chi Sao should become as close to real fighting as it can be made to be. I realize folks in the civilized, PC martial arts schools of today would be horrified and run away at the thought and teaching that "CHI SAO SHOULD BE SO HARD AND DIFFICULT THAT IT MAKES ACTUAL FIGHTING EASY AND FAST". Most pansy assed commercial martial arts students won't want to put in the time, effort and most of all pain it takes to get really good at Chi Sao. Once they realize the true amount of effort, sweat and pain Chi Sao takes - they drop the system.

DJ: Relaxation is one of the main ingredients to successful Ving Tsun however it is difficult to achieve while in action, meaning fighting or in Chi Sao. According to your understanding, why do you suppose this is and could you explain the personal method of how to achieve it?

WW: Relaxing during a fight comes from having learned the mindset that "Done with Little Thinking" (Sil Lum Tao) should have taught. Sil Lum Tao tells us to let our actions be automatic from kinesthetic deeply learned and nerve pattern engraved responses. Developing such kinesthetic responses is the job of Chi Sao!

DJ: There is a continual debate on whether Ving Tsun uses internal power/energy vs. body structure/mechanics. What is your belief on this? Also, what are the differences between internal and external when applied to Chi Sao particularly and in Ving Tsun generally?

WW: Both; internal power, chi, cannot flow unless the structure and bio mechanics are good. Look at Tai Chi, absolutely shitty bio mechanics imitating animals and they don't get the chi needed to win fights till 12 to 20 years into the art! The genius of Wing Chun is that it combines the best of HUMAN bio mechanics ever put into an empty-handed marital art and by the end of the system Bil Ji and Luk Dim Pun Quan, adds the chi to top off the icing on the cake to create DOUBLE POWER. The closest bio mechanics to those of Ving Tsun are that of French Fencing, most especially foil.

Look at their use of the wrist, over the Italian fencing use of the forearm, a Ving Tsun parry vs a karate block. Look at the parries in 4, 6 and 2 to see inside tan sao, outside tan sao and bong sao. Look at their reposts from those positions to see the instant counter response we do faster with two hands instead of fencings just one. As *X files* says "The Truth Is Out There", and the truth is that great biomechanics leading to great power and speed can and have been discovered / developed by man, but it is found in very few places!

DJ: Do you personally have any preferred training methods that develop the internal aspect?

WW: Drawing in chi during Sil Lum Tao, hands moving out while breathing out push's chi out, hands moving in while breathing in draws energy into you.

Toes in stance brings energy up from the earth, a toe out in a fighting stance as in 2nd form, allows you to send chi down the leg to anchor or kick. Also, of great help is developing Iron Palm, Iron Fist, Iron Fingers and doing the Shaolin chi drawing and projecting exercises.

DJ: At what stage were you introduced to Chi Gerk and what were the stages it was taught in?

WW: Started during Chum Kiu and continued into Bil Ji.

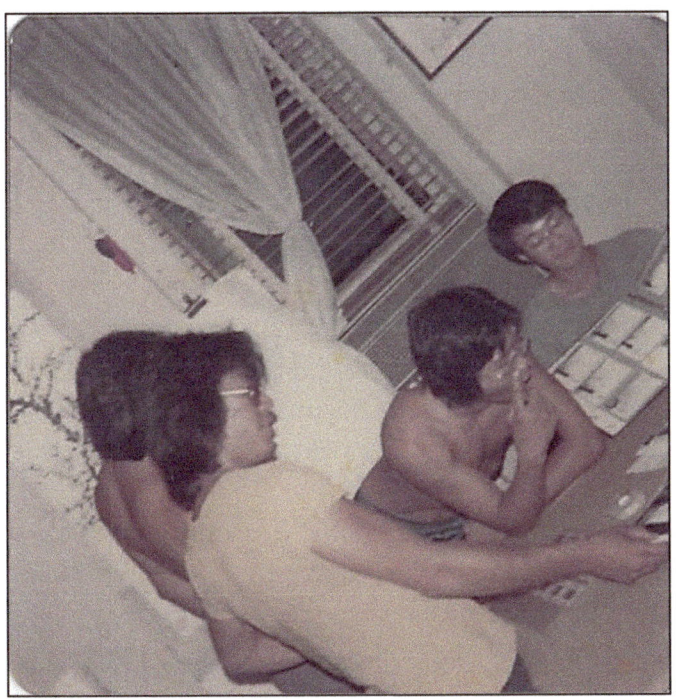

DJ: Did you reach the stage wherein training consisted of simultaneous Chi Gerk and Chi Sao and if so, do you recall who introduced it to you?

WW: Yes. Eddie Soto.

Eddie Soto

DJ: Most everyone in martial arts understands kicking targets e.g.; to the body and head, what advantages does Chi Gerk play in this regard, how is it used relating to a street fight?

WW: It's actual application against a moving dynamic opponent instead of rote kicking drills where there is no counter force or opposition or just empty kicking which is good to practice form with but not applicable to real fighting.

DJ: Do you recall any supplemental conditioning exercises or training methods that your Sifu taught that is not normally associated with Ving Tsun, which ones and for what reasons was your favorite?

DJ: Moy believed that Wing Chun provided all the conditioning one needed to fight with. I think that was one of his differences of opinion with Duncan Leung. While I always disagreed with the notion that one needed Ving Tsun alone and so did the best real fighters at our school. It has to be said that in the entire world there are no better conditioned fighters than college wrestlers. Period. Train for anaerobic (not aerobic capacity) because that's what you use in a fight. Train for dynamic strength and flexibility, as Olympic lifters and gymnasts do, not static strength and stiffness as body builders do; (remember that body building is a non-contact sport)! Even before your Sifu takes you there, if he ever does, train for Iron Palm and Iron Fist. Learn the Shaolin ways of chi gathering and projection. Practice Chi Sao till the cows come home, and it naturally gets put altogether!

DJ: Many of the traditional Chinese Sifu prefers not to work out with their students. Do you recall if your Sifu had ever worked out with students or with you and if so, what do you recall of the experience?

WW: Moy rarely worked out with us or taught us directly. Once Sifu promised to be with us either demonstrating during practice or sitting observing and commenting and correcting. That lasted 2 classes before he went back into his water color painting. Even though we were his disciples he taught as Yip Man did, by delegating. Most of what Moy learned he got taught and reviewed by Sibok Wong Shun Leung.

DJ: What about the mental aspect of fighting in the street, what needs to be foremost in the mind and is there any method you use to train this?

WW: All worry and doubt need to be put away and focus on the situation with an empty mind. MOST of the really good gung fu men I've known, including one or more of my CBC and ABC Sihing's have had their asses handed to them on the street because when push came to shove, they got emotional and they forgot their gung fu! Imagine that, getting so taken by the situation that you forget your gung fu! Also, smile at your enemy, especially if he pulls a blade and you present yours; it's very disconcerting to them!

DJ: Today in Ving Tsun, there are so many variations taught even among those from the same Sifu, is there any reason why you suppose this to be so?

WW: Ving Tsun considers itself to be an evolving art, that's what Moy taught; but he also added that it had evolved as far as it could go in what he was teaching. We all add our strengths and dislikes to our teaching of Ving Tsun and as with the apostles of Jesus all hearing the same message but understanding it differently one from another, we have much the same effect in Ving Tsun. I've heard from my grand students what my students said they heard me say and it's like boys playing a game of telephone. The message gets garbled or distorted entirely somewhere along the way.

DJ: In your experience, is there anything lacking in regards to Ving Tsun training or the philosophy thereof?

WW: We need more emphasis on the Iron chi training techniques.

DJ: What is your idea on cross training in Ving Tsun, do you think it's a good thing or even necessary?

WW: My Sihing Kenny would approve as he was a heavy weight college wrestler and Tang Soo Do black belt along with being an excellent Ving Tsun man. He would use whatever was appropriate in a real fight. I would tend to disagree especially as to the ground work because grappling an opponent on the street will get you stabbed, beaten or just plain killed by the rest of your opponent's friends. Cowards always attract in packs.

DJ: In your opinion, is there anything else other than for fighting that you believe Ving Tsun can be used for?

WW: Healing, but only if the iron and chi drawing techniques are learned to be able to draw and project chi. Moy Yat was also a Dit Da, (i.e. Hit Medicine), doctor and while showing us the special secret texts, said he could also do Dim Mak. I did not doubt that.

DJ: From the time you began training in Ving Tsun, how has it evolved from when you started, what are the differences from then and now?

WW: From the 1970's to now with the commercialization of the art we went from being among maybe 5000 to 10,000 of the toughest bad asses on earth, who could single handedly destroy any MoFo in "The Valley" to the meek and mild milk sop, tea toting pitiful excuse for a "martial" sport or activity I see taught in most of the Ving Tsun schools I've had the sorry experience to visit or look into. There might be some closed door and maybe even some open-door schools that still teach real Ving Tsun, but those are damn few. Among the great schools still available I list in Atlanta GA: Jason Lau, Francis Fong and Eddie Camden (the top most scariest good VT fighter I've EVER SEEN, though he's now mostly teaching BJJ and teaching Ving Tsun only to a few closed-door type students) and Duncan Leung's school in Virginia Beach. It needs to be said that even the great Duncan Leung tried to revive REAL Ving Tsun in China as they were losing national pride by losing full contact matches mostly to south east Asian fighters. He admits in his book "Wing Chun Warrior" that today's children are too soft to learn hard combat, a worry shared by the way by the Red Chinese Army as the boys of the "one child" policy in China are a soft, spoiled and moly coddled bunch with nowhere near the inner strength of their grandfathers and much less their great grandfathers. It's just about the same situation here in the West but for different reasons.

DJ: Do you believe that with all of the various VT lineages now known, along with their various understanding of what it is, do

GM Moy Yat - Ding Leg School *Ca.* 1975

you feel Ving Tsun will ever come under one roof, if not, please explain why in either case?

WW: No, why should they; Ving Tsun is not a religion with a set dogma, it's an art and as an art subject to differences in interpretation
and application. Confining it to a committee developed rote, would further ruin the 'art' and give away an individual's power to some small "elite or exclusive" group.

DJ: As we get older, Ving Tsun becomes more challenging to train for obvious reasons, how best should older practitioners train in this case?

WW: As one trying to train past, a severely worn right humeral head, from too many decades of Chi Sao and punching and inch punching bags of sand and rocks nailed onto trees, spinal stenosis, more spinal injuries herniations and fractures than I care to count and a few other ravages of having had an exciting life; I've tried to keep the iron skills up most because those will be the ones I use if the two Glock's and 357 Sig I carry along with the Voorhies bowie ever fail me.

DJ: There are those who believe they should pass down Ving Tsun exactly the way they learned it and others who have modified it according to their evolved understanding of it. Do you feel teaching one's personal modified Ving Tsun detracts from the original Ving Tsun ancestors teaching methods or do you feel this is suitable and a natural progression for the furtherance of Ving Tsun in the future?

WW: Everyone else who's taught Ving Tsun including Yip Man and Jiu Wan modified the art to their understanding or liking, why should future generations of Ving Tsun artists be enjoined from thinking, feeling and applying as they see or feel is fit?

DJ: How do you see Ving Tsun evolving in the future?

WW: Commercialism will kill the effectiveness of the art. Going back to closed door teaching aiming to train hard core fighters will revive it.

DJ: Is there any final advice or anything at all you would like to say for those of us in Ving Tsun that you would like to impart?

WW: Train hard, condition yourself hard in mind, spirit and body and work to BRING BACK the spirit of INVINCIBILITY Ving Tsun has always had before these days of commercialization.

DJ: Before we end, did you know Lee Moy Shan at that time when you were in the school, he had opened a school in Manhattan when you had joined?

WW: Yes, I knew Doug from Mr. K's Goshindo Kempo classes at the old International Schools of Self Defense on Church Ave. He was very senior to me. He was a brown belt going on black while I was still yellow and John Cheng was green or also brown. Jerry Mackie's judo school was right across the street at Flatbush and Church so there was always bad blood and ill feelings between the two schools, but I did not know that Doug taught there.

    Doug didn't visit Sifu at Ding Leg very often, that I can remember, and that I recall he only crossed hands with the senior brothers like John Cheng and Eddie Soto when he crossed hands at all. And yes, when I came into the family, Doug already had his school open in Manhattan.

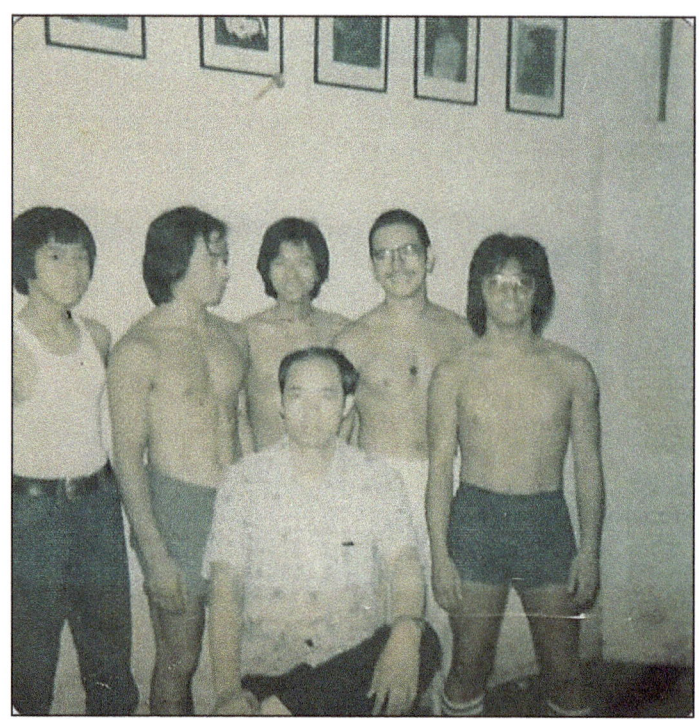

Ding Leg School Group Shot – William Wong second from right.

DJ: Do you recall the local commercial on T.V. Lee Moy Shan was the performer in it for the Mackey Studios, he was doing a praying mantis form, he studied with Gin Foon Mark?

WW: I do remember that TV commercial, guess I didn't notice it was Doug. Didn't know he studied with Mark!

Thank you, Dr. Wong.

About the Author

Sifu Darrell Jordan started training in boxing in 1967 while growing up in NYC. In 1968 he began training in Shotokan Karate with Sensei Charlie Zayas at the basement of St. James Church in Chinatown. Sifu Jordan had the opportunity to train in Okinawa and the Philippines in 1973 while he served with the United States Marine Corps. After returning to NYC in 1975, he subsequently began training at the Lee Moy Shan Ving Tsun Kung Fu School in 1977 and began assisting with instruction in 1978. In 1980 he was the day instructor when the school moved to Chambers St. In 1981 Sifu Jordan and his Sihing Steve Goericke went to open the first Ving Tsun School in New Hampshire, after establishing the school he moved back to NYC in 1982.

Darrell was accepted as a Disciple in 1985. Sifu Darrell has subsequent training in Ch'ang Tai Chi Chuan and Shuai Chiao while exchanging systems with his good friend Sifu Rocky Byars. After the death of Sifu Byar's, Sifu Jordan joined the International Shuai-Chiao Association headed by Grandmaster Gene Chicoine. Sifu Jordan has been involved in promoting the Chinese Martial Arts and officiates at National and International Chinese Martial Art Tournaments. Sifu Jordan is the Founder and President of the World Ving Tsun Association where he teaches publicly and privately.

World Ving Tsun.com
WVTA.us

"If You Do Not Train Hard When You Are Young, Then When You Are Old You Will Have Nothing."

Lee Moy Shan by Adam Chow

GM Chu Shong Tin school visiting Yip Man Grave with Buick Yip.

Photo's GM Chan shared with me.

Chan Chee Man with Andrew Ma and their Sihing Mo Kee

WVTA – HK, 1985

L-R; Tong Sing Chi, Pang Chi Yam, Tong Cho Chi, Yip Ching, Chan Chee Man, Andrew Ma

Chan Chee Man with Chan Kin Man

Chan Kin Man 2012 End of Year Gathering

2016 - Eric Wong Hosted dinner for Derick Fung (Far Left)

2013, L-R; Tom Tang, Chan Nuen Lam, Lee Wai Chi, Andrew Ma, Wong Hon Chung, Chan Chee Man, Chan Kin Man

Law Bing 80th birthday celebration

2018 - Judy Chan, Chan Kin Man, Chan Chee Man

2018 – Chan Chee Man at dinner with Wong Long, left of CCM.

L-R; Roland Tong, Andrew Ma, Chan Chee Man, Tong Shing

1983 - Lee Moy Shan School Photo

C. 2014, L-R; William Moy, Lee Moy Shan, Moy Cheng Four, Steve Goericke, David Robinson, Vinny Thomas, Author

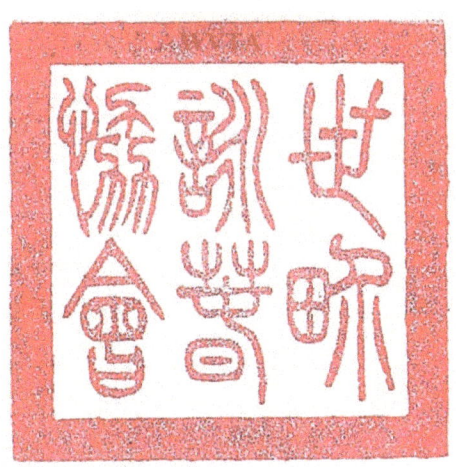

Other Products by the Author

Sifu Darrell Jordan
World Ving Tsun Association

- ∞ Training Programs
- ∞ Private Training
- ∞ Self-Study Video Programs
- ∞ Books

More information about the author, books, products and programs can be found at:

World Ving Tsun.com
WVTA.us

www.ingramcontent.com/pod-product-compliance
Lightning Source LLC
Chambersburg PA
CBHW050729010526
44107CB00009B/786